It's All About a Story

Be Encouraged

It's All About a Story

Be Encouraged

Dr. Frank McMeen

Copyright ©2023 by Dr. Frank McMeen

All rights reserved. No part of this book may be reproduced or utilized in any form or by any means, electronic or mechanical, including photocopy, recording, or by an information storage and retrieval system, without permission in writing from the publisher.

ISBN: 979-8-9888614-4-7

Printed and bound in the United States of America by Ingram Lightning Source

Edited by: Jacque Hillman, Kim T. Stewart, Katie Gould
Layout and design by: Kim T. Stewart
Cover photo by: Wanda Stanfill
Chapter art by: Jacque Hillman

The HillHelen Group LLC
470 North Parkway, Suite C
Jackson, TN 38305

The HillHelen Group LLC
635 North 65th Place
Mesa, AZ 85205

(731) 394-2894
www.hillhelengrouppublishers.com
hillhelengroup@gmail.com

Dedication

This book is dedicated
to my brother, Mike, and his wife, Jacquelyn,
who are among the best people I know.
I love them dearly.

Acknowledgments

Tennyson said, "I am a part of all I have met." My life continues to be impacted by so many.

Jamie and Scott Gatlin are wonderful friends and spiritual mentors. Many of the concepts in this book are from discussions that opened my eyes while we enjoyed coffee or a meal. Thank you for helping me see others through the eyes of Jesus.

Darren Lykes is a dear friend who, no matter what, lives a life showing love for others. He gives himself to so many causes that make positive impacts on lives of people whom he will never meet, believing that all lives are equally important and deserving of love.

Beth Koffman has been a coworker for nearly two decades. There is nothing she cannot do, and she proves that every day. I am a better person for having her as a friend and sounding board for all things important in our community.

Johnny Dodd, a fellow City Council member, exemplifies the concept of servant leadership. For decades, he has worked to improve some of our most vulnerable parts of this community. We are blessed by his commitment to all people.

My life has been a charmed one. My work brought impactful people into my life. Paul Harvey, Jane Seymour, Gary Morris, Vince Gill, Amy Grant, Tom Landry, Mary Lou Retton, Senator Howard Baker, Willard Scott, Barbara Bush, David Shannon, Vice President Dan Quayle, Milton Sewell, Dianne Odell, Brenda Lee, E. Claude Gardner, Libby Murphy, Billy Smith, and John Hall join many others.

Quoting two movies explains the charmed life I have enjoyed. From *Pretty Woman*, "I want it all . . . I want the fairy tale." To have that, you make many sacrifices, and because of such, my life has not been typical, it has been blessed. Clarence from *It's a Wonderful Life* was correct: "No man is a failure who has friends."

I am truly blessed. It is my hope that this book blesses you!

High Praise for
It's All about a Story

"Uplifting and food for the soul, Frank McMeen has fabulously weaved personal reflections, scripture, and short stories together to inspire readers to look for the common good, believe in themselves, and trust God whenever in doubt. The result of his work is a masterpiece in self-motivation and self-determination.

"Following McMeen on social media, I felt I knew his ninety-year-old father. But while reading the story about his dad, I found myself drifting back to my own childhood and working alongside my father and remembering those classic one-liners that only those who have life experiences can speak.

"*It's All about a Story* is not just a book, it is a call to action to help and love all people, regardless of background, education, and title."

—***Dr. Charley Deal**, vice chancellor for advancement at the University of Tennessee Foundation Inc.*

"Frank McMeen's second book, *It's All about a Story*, offers inspiration through everyday stories and anecdotes such as a drunk jumping from a second-story ledge, a walk with a university president, a conversation with a woman in an iron lung, or a community member suffering with cancer, just to mention a few. McMeen makes those stories relevant to lessons learned from biblical stories."

—***Niles Reddick**, author of the Pulitzer-nominated novel* Drifting Too Far from the Shore, *three collections of short fiction, and a novella. His work has been featured in over thirty collections and five hundred magazines and literary journals including* The Saturday Evening Post, New Reader Magazine, *and* Vestal Review.

"Frank McMeen is a masterful storyteller and the epitome of an encourager. In this collection of stories, he takes us on excursions, introducing us to people and places, immediately drawing us closer to the greatest story. Prepare to smile, laugh, and even cry. However, by the end of each story, expect to be encouraged."

—**David R. Shannon,** *president at Freed-Hardeman University*

"Compelling, poignant, and inspiring are my descriptions for *It's All about a Story* by Dr. Frank McMeen.

"A faithful Christian, and a Bible scholar, although he would dispute that, Frank tells his own stories and reflects on Bible stories. He embraces the power of the stories from the Bible, especially the stories of Jesus to lead us through to God's love, and heralds the power of love to change lives."

—**Shirley Raines,** *author and past president at University of Memphis*

FOREWORD

Be Uplifted, and Pay It Forward

There are few people in our lives who make us better. Frank McMeen is one of those individuals who brings out the best in everyone he is around. I met Frank in 1987 when I began my first real job after college graduation. He trained me in the new job, but more importantly, he taught me to value people and friendships. He has no idea of the impact he had on my life as a young professional. I am thankful for his friendship.

Frank has spent his life valuing people and helping them reach their potential. He spent many years in Christian education and is now serving through his work at the Community Foundation of West Tennessee.

Frank has a gift as a storyteller. He can relate everyday experiences to greater principles. His love for people is outweighed only by his love for God.

You will be encouraged by reading *It's All about a Story*. Frank takes things that happen each day and relates them to teachings in the Bible. These stories will encourage you to be a better son or daughter, parent, brother, sister, employee, and friend. You will be amazed at the lessons to be learned from Frank's life. Once you begin reading the book, you will find it hard to put down. I encourage you to take the lessons from the book and apply them to your life to be a better person. The world needs more people who will have a positive influence on our society.

We tend to forget that the people of the Bible were real people. They were flesh, just like us. We can learn more from them when we realize that they were human. This book brings these people to life. Each story has a message that reminds us that God is not done with us yet. He knows best, and we struggle to understand that. God can use the smallest things to teach us powerful lessons. This is shown throughout the book.

Frank has invested in the lives of many people and made them better. Sometimes we don't have any idea of the impact we make on others. May we all be able to encourage the people with whom we interact after reading *It's All about a Story*. It takes an investment on our part to make a difference, but the investment is worth it. Do it today!

—***Dr. Wayne Scott,*** *executive vice president at Bethel University*

Table of Contents

Chapter 1: The Dichotomy of God	1
Chapter 2: A Table for Two	7
Chapter 3: Dad Is Ninety	11
Chapter 4: My Hometown	21
Chapter 5: Homecoming	25
Chapter 6: Love Sees Us Through	35
Chapter 7: It's All about Power	39
Chapter 8: The President Came to Town	53
Chapter 9: Neighbors	65
Chapter 10: Hold onto Them Tightly	77
Chapter 11: Communion	83
Chapter 12: If I Just Had Power	91
Chapter 13: Extravagance	99
Chapter 14: The Life of the Party	103
Chapter 15: Alone at a Train Station	115
Chapter 16: An Iron Lung and a Storm	123
Chapter 17: The Ash Heap	133
Chapter 18: Troubled Times	139
Chapter 19: You May Remember Mark	143
Chapter 20: Has God Spoken to You?	151
About the Author	157

"Jesus told His disciples to live differently, to live opposite of what the world expects."

CHAPTER 1

The Dichotomy of God

We were running late. I was walking with a university president, on the way to an important banquet featuring a famous guest speaker.

He had been president of Freed-Hardeman University for years. Nearing retirement, he was highly respected and loved.

I gently urged him to walk a little faster.

As we walked into the banquet venue, he saw some water on the floor. I made a mental note to call someone to mop up the water, *after* I had the president in his seat at the head table.

My plan didn't work. The president darted to the left and opened a storage closet. Mop in hand, he said, "Frank, grab those towels." We were cleaning up someone else's disaster.

With the spill cleaned, I quickly put the mop and towels away and thanked the president for his alertness.

This highly intelligent college president was like my grandfather. He recruited me from Columbia, Tennessee, when I was in high school and hired me to work at the university shortly after I graduated from there. At this point, I was in my twenties.

We were on our way to the banquet hall for a dinner with William F. Buckley Jr., the widely known conservative writer and political commentator. He was meeting with students. The president and I were behind schedule and my job was to get him to the banquet hall in record time.

As we finally got on the elevator and headed for the banquet, the president continued to mentor me.

"Frank, I couldn't walk by and leave whatever was spilled on the floor not to be addressed," he said.

"I understand, sir," I responded.

With that powerful lesson, I escorted him to the head table.

This was not the first time I saw the president take on the role of the janitor. In fact, I don't know why I seemed to be around him when he took on other roles. Often, he became the groundskeeper, picking up paper on the campus lawns.

He never complained. He would just find the mop or pick up the paper and never notify housekeeping or groundskeeping. The top of the food chain became what is sometimes thought of as the bottom of the food chain.

The head guy took on the opposite role, a real dichotomy.

I am amazed at the dichotomy of God.

That is a big word simply meaning "opposites."

The opposites are important.

The opposites are critical.

The opposites are true, proving the point.

All my life, I grew up with the understanding that drinking was a sin. If you drank one drink, you were "one-drink drunk," and God condemned drinking.

Yet at a wedding in Cana of Galilee, Jesus turned water into wine. The best of wine.

That doesn't seem to fit the "one-drink drunk" concept.

Jesus was a man of dichotomies.

God makes a point of taking a dead man and giving him life.

God uses a teetotaler to announce the Savior, who with His first miracle turns water to wine.

We go from John the Baptist, a teetotaler who recently announced that Jesus, the Son of God, was walking down a street in Jerusalem, to Jesus turning water into wine as His very first miracle.

Opposites, beginnings, and endings.

Wine at a wedding and whips at the Temple.

Elizabeth being pregnant with John the Baptist and having the baby at an elderly age.

Mother and son.

Mary and Jesus.

Earthly and Divine.

Elizabeth and John.

God sent word by an angel to Elizabeth's husband that he and his wife would have a child. Imagine how she felt, having lost hope for a child of her own. Imagine if she had been the one to talk to the angel Gabriel.

"Elizabeth, I am Gabriel, and I have been sent to let you know that you are going to bear a child."

"No, I'm not! I am not going to have a child. I am old. You don't have children when you are old."

"Elizabeth, I am sent from God. In your old age, you will have a child."

"God has a need to show a young lady His power."

"God will use you so that you will become a sign to others. God needs you."

"God needs me?"

"Yes, God needs to show that He can use a woman past birthing years and show that she, by the power of God, can have a child.

"Elizabeth, this dichotomy in your life will show that the impossible can happen.

"It will show a young girl that God will use her just as He is using you."

Imagine being a fly on the wall when the angel visited a doubtful Zechariah:

"Zechariah, your wife Elizabeth is going to have a child."

"No, she isn't."

"Yes, she is. Zechariah, your prayer has been heard."

"Which prayer?"

"The one where you were praying for children."

"Prayers for children? I did that decades ago."

"Yes, you did . . . and God heard those prayers."

"Isn't it kind of late to be answering that prayer now? Elizabeth and I are very old."

"No, the timing is perfect."

"What do you mean the timing is perfect? The timing stinks!"

"This is the perfect time for you to have a child with Elizabeth."

"You may be an angel, but you must not know how humans have children. At some point, you are too old to have children."

"Yes, Zechariah, that is correct. Not only will you have a child, but you will have him in your old age. God needs you, even when it doesn't make sense, because that is when it makes the *most* sense . . . and you'll name him John."

"We don't have any Johns in our family. That is not a family name. Even if we were to have a child, his name would not be John."

"Your son will be named John."

"What proof do you have that this is going to happen?"

"What proof? Do you not know that I am Gabriel? I stand before God. I have come to tell you this truth. Your son, John, will proclaim the Savior to the world. He will proclaim the Word, but you will not be able to speak until he is born. John will preach the Good News, and you will be silent."

Zechariah was dumbfounded, shocked into disbelief.

Now picture the dichotomy of Mary's faith when presented with similar news.

"Mary, you are highly favored by the Lord."

"What? And who are you? What are you doing here?"

"Mary, you have found favor with God."

"Who am I to be favored by God?"

"Mary, the Lord needs you. You will have a child. You, of humble birth, will have a child who will be great."

"Sir, I know how babies come into the world. I have not done what it takes to have a baby."

"That may be the case, but you will become pregnant."

"There is no way that I can have a baby, because I haven't been with someone in that way. It's impossible."

"Mary, as proof, you will find that your elderly cousin, who could not get pregnant, is having a child in her old age."

This dichotomy of God is amazing.

The young child David slew a nine-foot giant.

The young man Joseph was sold into slavery and ended up controlling a nation.

Paul, who breathed out hate and destruction to the early church, became the powerful spokesperson for church after church.

Even the teachings are dichotomies.

"The dead shall be raised."

"The crooked places will be made straight."

The most powerful dichotomy was when Jesus, knowing what was about to happen, gathered His disciples in the Upper Room. They prepared for a meal but received a most powerful message.

Jesus knew that the Father had put *all* things under His power.

Here was Jesus, knowing who He was—Creator of the world, God in the form of man, the perfect reflection of God—getting up from the meal, taking off His outer clothing, and wrapping a towel around His waist. Jesus did what servants usually did.

We have a problem when we see people step outside of their roles. Peter had that problem.

"Lord, you want to wash my feet? You will never wash my feet!"

"Peter, you don't understand this now, but later you will. If you won't let me wash your feet, you won't have any part of me."

What?

"Lord, then wash not only my feet—wash my hands and my head as well!"

Jesus continued around the room, foot after foot after foot.

"Now that I have washed your feet . . . you are to wash my feet." That's what we'd expect.

If I scratch your back, you scratch my back. Or someone else's back. Sounds right. It fits into most cultures. That's what most people expect.

That's not exactly how He said it, though. He actually told His disciples to wash *one another's* feet. If the Lord humbles Himself in service to others, so should His followers.

We assume something Jesus never intended.

It is interesting that Jesus never told His disciples to fight culture. Jesus never told His disciples to take on campaigns to fight culture. Jesus simply told His disciples to live differently, to live opposite of what the world expects.

Not fight.

Not yell.

Not boycott.

Live opposite of what the world expects.

You will be light in a world of darkness.

You will be yeast expanding into the entire loaf.

You will be a city set on a hill that cannot be hidden.

When others compel you to go a mile, go with them two.

If someone strikes you on the cheek, turn the other cheek.

If people hate you, you are to love them.

With all our knowledge and technology, we seem to miss the simple way to greatness. Instead of throwing in the towel, pick up the towel.

He who will be the greatest must also be a servant.

CHAPTER 2

A Table for Two

He walked into a downtown restaurant and the hostess greeted him. "How many in your party?"

"I would like a table for two."

That night was life-changing.

A casual meeting, a week earlier, created a spark.

There was dinner at a downtown restaurant. The dinner started early, but on this Wednesday night, the two looked around as their dinner was winding down and saw the restaurant was nearly empty.

Every other customer had left.

The staff was even putting chairs on the tables.

They had known each other for a while. In fact, the two had dated for a short while nearly a decade earlier. There had been no spark back then.

Bells didn't ring and birds didn't sing that first time.

This time seemed different.

For hours, the two talked and ate, never noticing other customers or what was going on around them.

They were totally consumed at their table for two. Neither expected the outcome. Two days later, it was dinner again. Then Saturday night, a concert. Countless texts and phone calls. Flowers came that next Wednesday, arriving at work on the anniversary of that initial dinner. And the anniversaries didn't stop. Flowers arrived every Wednesday.

It sounds like a romance novel—without the cheesy, sexy cover art of some shirtless guy flexing in front of a beautiful sunset. You know that stuff that is not real.

Love is strange in how it works, because it is not always romantic. Acts of love are being performed all around the world millions of times a day.

In poverty-stricken Sierra Leone, Africa, countless acts of kindness are happening.

Dr. Jimmy Kamso-Pratt grew up in a cardboard house in a Sierra Leone garbage dump where the city's sewage ran into the Atlantic Ocean. He escaped poverty after moving to the United States and becoming a physician.

Eventually, he started a clinic to treat the poor.

There was no big house or fancy car. Dr. Pratt lived in a small house and drove an old sedan that needed a bath and a wax. He saved the income that he made as a hospitalist to send back to help the poor in his home city in Africa.

His patients there had no money to pay for any services. He purchased expired US medicine. Even past the expiration date, it was better than no medicine.

We visited Sierra Leone together, and he arranged for lunch with the country's vice president. We arrived at Sierra Leone's most exclusive restaurant. As we walked in, the hostess asked, "How many in your party?"

"I need a table for two," Dr. Pratt responded.

With that, Dr. Pratt looked at me, making sure that I understood. Business would be conducted at this lunch. He was on a mission to get medicine from America to the poorest people of Sierra Leone.

He didn't need a guy who didn't speak the language. He didn't need a guy who didn't know the people, one who might get the conversation sidetracked due to the novelty of being an American. He didn't need me distracting the vice president just by being present.

That day, I ate lunch in a fancy Sierra Leone restaurant with the driver, while Dr. Pratt met with the vice president. I don't remember the driver's name. I'm sure he didn't remember mine.

At a table for two, Dr. Pratt was so entrenched in business that he hardly knew what was going on around them.

Every day, a table for two is effective in business, romance, reunions, friendships. But there is another presence that is quite different. This dinner guest is global.

Around the world, people gather around a table for two . . . each Sunday.

It's not a romantic dinner, nor a business lunch.

Of all the gatherings, this "table for two" is perhaps the most impactful.

It happened today. I was sitting in a room with hundreds while at my table for two.

It was a really simple table, nothing fancy.

The meal was simple: bread and juice.

Others were at a similar meal, all over this globe.

At each table was simply one person and Jesus.

Everyone had the same simple meal: bread and juice.

Today's purpose was simple—remembering what He did, not anything we had done.

Around the world, "tables for two" have been sparked by what happened two thousand years ago.

While this table was for two . . . it is a table for all.

This table is reserved for all His children.

Everyone who is a child of God can sit at this table. It doesn't matter about skin color, net worth, sexuality, nation of origin, Republican, Democrat, or even Communist.

This table is for *all*.

As we take of the Lord's Supper, we treat that bread honorably in that it represents the body of Christ that was broken for us.

The Apostle Paul made three notations:

1) His body was broken for you.
2) You must "examine yourself."
3) You must discern the Lord's body.

We would have difficulty accepting someone taking that wafer and tossing it on the floor and crushing it with their foot. Doing something like that would dishonor what that bread stood for.

That bread is the body, and we would not tolerate someone disrespecting the body of Christ.

While we have that sense of respect for a wafer, you cannot honor the wafer and then dishonor the body of Christ—those who make up the body of Christ . . . His church.

Let us remember that this is His table. And those of us who gather around His table are His brothers and sisters.

The things that divide us in the world are not things that divide us around this table. At this table, barriers cease to exist. In a world of billions, it's still a table for two.

At this table, He still shares a truth. A truth that nothing, absolutely nothing, can separate you from His love that brought you to the table in the first place.

"It is the gift of God, not of works, lest any should boast."

Thanks be to God for this unspeakable gift.

CHAPTER 3

Dad Is Ninety

You can get into some interesting conversations with an energetic ninety-year-old, like my dad.

We have talked about the celebration we will have when he turns one hundred.

I tell him that my friends think he is Superman.

He manages the farm. He deals with trees when they fall on fences. Fences are important when you have cattle. When a limb or tree falls on a fence, he removes the tree and repairs the fence.

He raises and sells cattle. He feeds the cows, pulls the calves (you may not know what that is . . . and if you don't, I won't tell you). When they go through a fence row, my ninety-year-old father goes and finds them and brings them back to the farm. They may be on another farm or down the road or who knows where, but he finds them and brings them back.

Dad has three gardens. He bales his own hay and even bales hay on other people's farms.

The list of things that Dad does is unending.

Oh, another thing Dad does is nap. He does get his naps in.

They may be at church, or watching the news, or sitting on the porch. Naps are important when you are ninety.

"I need to tell you what happened," Dad said, and I wondered whether this would be funny or serious.

It was serious.

The day before, he hooked the big auger (a large drill that you use to drill holes in the ground) onto the back of one of his tractors. He was on his way to replace the fencing around the barn.

The fence was older and the posts holding up the gate were old and rotting. His goal was to keep certain cows that he is about to sell close to the barn.

So he had hooked up the auger and was walking behind it. For some reason, the hydraulics gave way and the auger came down—*on Dad.*

Hitting his neck and shoulder, it knocked him down and pinned him under the massive drill on the ground.

For a while, he was all alone, under the auger.

Being Superman, Dad worked himself out from under it and raised it back up. Despite being in pain, he went and replaced the posts that held the gate in place.

What do you say? I was in shock. I cannot imagine that massive posthole digger falling on me and pinning me down.

"Did you go to the doctor?"

"No, it only hit my neck and shoulder. It's better today," he said, *five days later.*

Dad is of another generation—born during the Depression and raised in the country. It was different back then. My grandmother made clothes for Dad and his seven brothers and sisters.

He told me that one of his classmates passed away recently.

"I hate that!" I said. "How old was he?"

"Oh, he was a year or two older than me," he said, adding, "and he would make fun of me for being 'country' and wearing clothes that were made by my mother."

"This guy made fun of you for wearing homemade clothes?" I asked.

"Yes, he did, and he wasn't the only one. There were several who made fun of all of us who lived on farms and wore homemade clothes," Dad said.

"How old were you?"

"I was in elementary school. I guess that was about 1939. We just didn't have money for store-bought clothes, so Momma made them for us." That statement touched my heart.

People of Dad's generation raised their own food. They used mules to plow their fields. Going to school required walking more than a mile . . . just to catch the bus.

From his ninety-year-old perspective, he didn't quite understand the importance of an education beyond a basic four-year degree. I got that one, then a master's and a doctorate.

"Son, just how much education do you need?" Dad asked me on a couple of occasions.

From his perspective, a high school diploma was all you needed.

"I just need to get one more degree, Dad, which you are not paying for," I'd say with a grin.

This nonagenarian built his own business.

Won two world championships.

Built his own training facility for the horses.

Kept a small church alive.

Became an expert woodworker, making furniture and gifts for family and friends.

He taught his kids to work hard and be good people.

Taught his kids that you don't embarrass your family name.

Taught his kids to respect their elders.

Taught his kids to love and help their neighbors.

Taught his kids that they must love their country.

Taught his kids to be kind to animals . . . unless they are getting into your garden.

Taught his kids to be generous.

It was for this man, who had accomplished so much with so little, that it became important that I finish my doctorate.

It became highly important to me to place my dissertation in his hand.

He and my mother supported my education, even when they didn't understand why I needed it.

It became highly important that I publish at least one book.

I wrote my first book, *Let Me Tell You a Story*, so I could place a copy in my dad's hands and he could read the dedication to him and my mother.

How in the world could I measure up to such a man?

To me, completing a doctorate and writing a book was my effort to tell my father that I, too, can accomplish big things just like he did.

Today we are losing Dad's generation of greatness, as we have lost those previously.

All the talent, expertise, and wisdom is hard to pass on.

It is for those like my dad that brings to mind the statement of King David . . .

"I have been young, and now I am old. I have never seen the righteous forsaken nor his seed begging bread."

With all of this in mind, keep folks like my dad in your prayers.

They have lived through the Depression.

They have lived through the Vietnam War.

They saw social change that put races together.

They saw special-needs children having an education and much-needed therapy.

They saw economic booms and busts.

They started businesses and worked in factories.

They saw the start of credit cards and debit cards.

They lived through car "bag phones," flip phones, and iPhones.

We can find no better models for life.

We see no greater examples of success based on hard work.

We rarely see a stronger commitment to free enterprise.

We still see their belief in the power of the press.

They understand the power of Election Day and that the majority wins.

We are a better country because men like my dad continue to work and dream daily, sometimes alone, with their children far away . . . depending on God to be with them.

They are often the life of a party, and the stabilizing factor of a family.

Men and women like my dad are the vintage wine, the best wine. Vintage wine is exceptional.

At the beginning of His ministry, Jesus had been baptized by John the Baptist, then invited to a wedding.

Mary, Jesus, and His disciples were all invited to the wedding.

Weddings then were like weddings today. A lot of preparation goes into making the wedding flow: enough food, enough chairs, the right people, and often . . . wine.

We don't know how it happened—if there was a lack of planning, or people just drank a lot—but they ran out of wine!

Not only did they run out, but they ran out long before the planners or guests expected.

Word got to Mary.

This was a wedding celebration. Wine was part of the celebration. Running out of wine would definitely end the party. Maybe because she was a mother, she knew where to go. Mothers can fix most things.

Evidently, Mary knew of the problem before the guy in charge of the wedding knew.

Mary did what moms do; she fixed the problem. Mary walked up to Jesus, and I assume she whispered in Jesus's ear: "They have no more wine."

After her conversation with Jesus, Mary addressed the servers.

"Do whatever He tells you to do," she said, and walked away.

Jesus, being put on the spot, looked around at six large water pots. "Uhhh . . . take those water pots and fill them with water."

Those water pots were there for another purpose. That day, those containers took on a whole new role.

Saying nothing more than to fill the pots with water, Jesus told the servers to take the new wine to the master of the wedding.

Jesus didn't wave His hands over the pots.

Jesus didn't say some magical words.

Jesus just said, "Take this cup to the master of the wedding."

Not knowing anything, the wedding master drank from the cup and remarked how good the wine was. He walked over to the bride and groom and complimented them on the wine.

"You have kept the vintage wine until now. How impressive!"

There are various levels of wine.

There is Boone's Farm 2019, and then there is Chateau Cheval Blanc 1947. With those two wines, there is probably a $340,000 price difference.

Then there are the pots. Each held twenty to thirty gallons of water. Just estimating, that would be somewhere close to one thousand bottles of wine today.

If the pots were filled with Chateau Cheval Blanc 1947, there would be a value for that one wedding of a little over $340 million.

John notes that the disciples saw this miracle and believed that Jesus was the Messiah.

This was Jesus's first miracle. A celebration. The beginning of a family.

This was life-changing for the disciples.

When I read this story of Jesus's first miracle, I have a personal connection.

For most of us, life is like the wedding.

We are young and in love. Life is good. You can't wait to begin your life with your beloved!

You have the new job. The new house. The new car. The perfect vacation. Children are born.

It seems that our lives serve the best first, and then comes Boone's Farm.

Then comes the inferior, the deficient.

The thrill! The excitement! The party! Becomes the lame.

The party has now run out of wine.

Have you ever noticed how families get excited when someone is expecting a baby?

Every family loves a new baby. Naming the child! What a special time.

Once there was a greatly anticipated birth. The child was born and the world celebrated. Angels announced it from the heavens. Very wise men came from the East, looking for the great king.

The child was born ever so humbly, yet announced so regally.

The wise men even went to Herod, asking about the birth of the king. Their encounter with Herod was a plot twist. They announced the birth, but then . . . then the party ran out of wine.

The party ended. Herod ordered all of the male children to be killed.

What do you do when you run out of wine?

What do you do when you are told, "They are out of wine?"

You make a decision: "Do I stay at a party with no wine . . . or do I go look for something more fun?"

You might dutifully stay at the party, or you follow your friends who are leaving.

Then someone goes to Jesus. Someone becomes the Mary.

Have you ever had friends rally around you in prayer?

Like the wedding master, you may never know who whispers to Jesus, "They have no wine."

Who is *your* Mary?

Mary knew Jesus. Since His miraculous birth, she knew. Mothers always know.

She simply knew who He was and whispered in His ear: "They have no wine."

You probably have all kinds of Marys around you, all of them whispering in His ear.

Maybe *you* are Mary, keeping the feast going. You go to the Master and whisper . . . *they have no wine.*

You tell the wedding servants: "Do whatever He tells you."

With that, servants begin to do what they have been told.

When someone whispers in Jesus's ear about your wedding feast—and the lack of wine that will destroy whatever is your wedding feast—your servants do what they have been told to do: pray, even fasting. They want to keep the party going.

Who are your water pots?

Perhaps you are the pots, filled to the brim with water turned into wine. The perfect wine to keep the party going.

Your water pots may be friends who have come back into your life. When you run out of wine, miracles never happen in the same way.

"Go wash in the Pool of Siloam."

"Go show yourself to the priests."

"Take up your bed and walk."

"Remove the stone."

"Fill the water pots to the brim."

Some people in your life will be like those water pots.

When you run out of wine, the miracle is not the filling of the pots. It's the change that happens within them. Jesus saw the pots and gave them a new purpose, to keep the party going.

You filled . . . He turned it to wine.

The people around you don't understand where the wine came from. They just know that the best wine continues to be poured.

What happened to you?

Most people serve the best at the beginning. But you are the best wine, at this point in your life.

Your best is now.

You can go from good wine to inferior wine. That's what most people do. Or you run out of wine altogether, waiting for a Mary.

The vintage is the best, the older.

You will run out of wine. You may be out of wine now. Please know that everyone runs out of wine.

Not everyone has a Mary to whisper in Jesus's ear.

Not everyone sees the pots waiting to be filled.

Jesus turns common water . . . that has been placed into pots . . . into the most extraordinary, vintage wine.

The world does not turn anything into vintage wine.

Be the Mary, and whisper in His ear.

Be the pots that are holding the best wine that will be shared at the wedding feast, as you become vintage.

Remember the words of the Psalmist, King David.

It's being whispered in your ear: "I have never seen the righteous forsaken, nor his seed begging bread."

Don't give up when you run out of wine.

Don't allow others to run out of wine.

Take a moment now and whisper in Jesus's ear that someone is out of wine.

*"The Spirit of the Lord is on me,
because He has anointed me
to proclaim good news to the poor."*

CHAPTER 4

My Hometown

I was born at a very young age in Columbia, Tennessee. There was a little humor in that statement—very little, but maybe enough to make you grin. My hometown was and is a great place to grow up.

When my brother and I were in the seventh grade, we went to a big school. We were big boys then. We tried to be cool.

Mom drove us to school a lot. Mom was big on kissing. Her teenage boys were not. Mom would pull up in front of the school, in front of our friends . . . and kiss us!

Oh, the embarrassment! We were grown up and cool.

"Mom, will you drop us off a block from school? We can walk from there!"

It was not cool for moms to drop off seventh-graders in front of the school. Mom was determined to pull right up to the front door, surely for no reason other than to embarrass us.

"Give me a kiss! Oh, I love you!"

We wanted to melt. We knew that the world heard our mom say those words and then kiss us in front of our friends.

She would get that red lipstick all over our cheeks.

It was a rough life growing up with our mom. She destroyed our "coolness." We knew we were doomed!

Surprisingly, we survived seventh grade and all that goes with adolescence.

Mom loved us.

We knew she did, but did she have to make it so public? Seventh-grade boys have a hard time dealing with moms who delight in kissing their children in front of their other "cool" friends.

Mom loved every minute of it. Every one of our friends' moms did the same thing.

Despite all those moms embarrassing their seventh-graders, we lived in a great hometown.

Everyone comes from somewhere. Our hometowns have a huge impact on our whole lives.

So many of my friends came from small towns. I don't know anyone who says their hometown is New York City or Los Angeles.

Hometowns make us who we are.

I have visited Jesus's hometown several times.

Nazareth was a small town. Jesus learned to read and write there. He learned scripture and began His first job there.

Mary had to be the same sort of mom that we had in my hometown. Perhaps Jesus said, "Mom, don't kiss me in front of my friends!"

I hope Mary kissed Him right in front of His friends. I hope Jesus was shy and kind of embarrassed when He attended a community event and had His first dance in His hometown.

I hope Jesus was on the ball field when the team captain kept picking others to be on the team and Jesus felt like He might not be picked.

Can you imagine the nervousness that Jesus and all His friends had when they were asked to read scripture or took part in the Sabbath meeting in the synagogue?

I grin when I think about Jesus as a ten-year-old kid, sitting with His buddies in the synagogue memorizing scripture.

Did Jesus, as a kid, know the scriptures already?

Whatever life was like in Nazareth, Jesus was part of it.

As a grownup, Jesus lived and worked as a carpenter. He made furniture and built houses. Then He left town.

He was a carpenter and the son of a carpenter. But Jesus the Carpenter changed careers and left His hometown. Jesus made a major career change: evangelist, preacher, teacher. Maybe He continued to do carpentry.

Then, one day, He came back to Nazareth.

Jesus returned on the Sabbath and went to the synagogue. The one He had grown up in.

It was there in front of all the folks who helped raise Him that Jesus read from Isaiah 61.

"The Spirit of the Lord is on me, because He has anointed me to proclaim good news to the poor."

". . . to set at liberty the captive."

". . . to give sight to the blind."

". . . to rescue the oppressed."

". . . to proclaim the year of the Lord."

Jesus handed the scroll back to the attendant and sat down.

The people were amazed at His teaching. *Where did this guy we grew up with receive such wisdom? We watched Him grow up here.*

They continued to be amazed and talk amongst themselves, until Jesus stood again and spoke.

"No prophet is accepted in his hometown," He said.

"There were many widows in Israel during the three years of drought, but God sent Elijah to a widow who was not an Israelite."

"There were many Israelites suffering from leprosy in the time of Elisha the prophet. Yet God sent Elisha to Naaman, a Syrian."

His hometown friends didn't know "this Jesus." This was a Jesus they couldn't accept. It was in their scripture but never preached on. "We are God's people, they are not," they believed.

"You're not really 'one of us' if you say these types of things."

His hometown friends couldn't accept that "this Jesus" was God's spokesperson.

Something happened on that Saturday in the synagogue.

That day, people who helped raise Jesus decided that they knew Jesus too well. God wouldn't send a guy they knew to teach them. That day, Nazareth's greatest advantage became their greatest stumbling block.

"We know him! He can't be the Messiah."

"Oh, we know Him too well. God is at work in the world, but not here in Nazareth, not through Him."

They believed God brought fire down from Heaven with Elijah. They believed God did big things—a long time ago, but not here, and not now, with someone they grew up with.

Columbia (or your hometown) is the hometown of Jesus. We have grown up with Him. We may believe He did great things elsewhere, but He's not doing things here. Not in our hometown.

He did unbelievable things with Moses and Elijah, but not with us in Columbia!

We have grown up knowing Jesus. We know all about Him.

May we never become the people of Nazareth.

Jesus had become so commonplace that they could not see the Messiah coming from among them.

Jesus was there, amazing them with His words, but they could not see God putting the Messiah right there with them.

Wherever you are, don't let Jesus become so commonplace that you cannot see that God is working and changing lives right there where you live . . . through people you know.

Lord, help us that we may accept Jesus as He works, right here.

Lord, we have grown up with Jesus, right here.

This is His hometown.

Let us see Him work.

CHAPTER 5

Homecoming

It was our senior year. We were on our way to school, taking Dad's truck for one of the floats in the homecoming parade. We broke down seven miles from school.

This was an important day. We were going to be pulling a homecoming float with a 1971 Ford F150. It was a great truck, but for some reason it died on the Hampshire Pike headed to Columbia. We were going to be late, if we made it at all.

We were stranded on the side of the road. This was before cell phones, so at seven thirty in the morning, this long-haired high school senior went up to the nearest house and knocked.

There was an older female voice on the other side of the door:

"What do you want?"

"Can I borrow your phone? Our truck broke down on the road and I need to call my parents."

"Where do you live?"

We lived on the other side of Cross Bridges.

"What is your name?" she asked.

"I'm Frank, and this is my brother Mike."

"Frank and Mike who?" the stranger asked.

Frank McMeen.

"Your name is Frank McMeen?"

"Yes, ma'am."

"Who is your grandfather?"

"My granddad is John McMeen."

What in the world? I thought. *Why is she asking all of these questions? All we want to do is use her phone.*

The questions continued.

"Who are your aunts and uncles?"

"Well, there's John and Taylor and Janie and Dell and Minnie Ruth . . ."

"Where does Taylor live?"

This is odd! I thought.

"Taylor lives in Florida."

With that, she opened the door.

"It's nice to meet you. Come on in and use the phone," she said. "I love your family, and I used to go to church with your grandparents before they moved to town. I lost my husband and now I live alone here."

I began to see why she had questions for long-haired kids knocking on her door.

Dad came to the rescue and found a clogged fuel line and fixed it. We thanked Dad and the lady at the door and were on our way, late but in time for the homecoming parade.

I never forgot the woman behind the door. "Who is your grandfather?"

I'm glad that she knew my family.

I'm not an answer-the-door person. If I'm not expecting you, I'm not opening the door no matter the hour.

Several years ago, a guy came to my door in the night. *Who is this at my door at two thirty in the morning?* I thought.

That night, I did go to the door, with my gun, and asked who he was. He made some strange comment I could not understand. My house was almost a hundred years old. It had a wide, solid wood door with beveled glass sidelights—glass panels—on each side. I put my pistol against the glass and said, "Do you see this?"

His hand went to the glass and he said, "I have one, too!"

He did have one!

Now I had a problem. His gun was different from mine. It was real. Mine was fake. I was always afraid I'd shoot someone, so I had a fake gun.

I pulled back my "gun." He did, too.

"Sir, you just need to go away," I said.

Luckily, he did. I don't go to the door at two thirty in the morning anymore.

The lady behind the door had a question. When I was the one behind the door, I asked the same one.

There are times when we all ask: "Who is this person?"

Remember when Moses saw the burning bush?

Moses saw the bush burning, but the bush was not burned. Moses and God had a discussion. "Who are you?"

"I want you to go to Pharaoh and bring my people back. I've heard their cries, and I want you to go bring them back."

Moses resisted, multiple times. God consoled him, "I will be with you."

"Who are you?"

It is funny that Pharaoh didn't ask who God was. Only God's people asked.

Just like the lady behind the door when I was in high school.

Just like me asking the guy at two thirty in the morning at my front door: "Who is this?"

Moses asked, "What do I say when I tell the Israelites, 'The God of your fathers has sent me,' and they ask, 'What is His name?'"

I didn't think it was odd that the lady behind the door asked who we were.

I'm sure the guy at my door at two thirty in the morning did not think it odd that I asked who he was.

Moses questioned God again.

"What do I tell them?"

Who is this God who sent me?

God gave Moses the most unique answer.

You tell them this God is "I AM."

God didn't say, "I am Jehovah, I am Yahweh."

He said, "You tell them, 'I AM.'"

Several years ago, I performed a wedding.

I had just returned from Africa and was very sick.

I went to the hospital's infectious disease doctor, who gave me a powerful medicine and told me to stay in bed.

I was lying in bed, not feeling good at all, when the phone rang.

"Where are you?" the voice said.

"Who is this—and where *should* I be?" I asked.

"This is Pam from the wedding chapel, and you have a wedding here in thirty minutes."

Yikes! I jumped in the shower, got dressed, and headed to the wedding chapel. I arrived about fifteen minutes late.

Pam handed me the marriage license. I wrote down the names and prepared for the wedding. Pam had shared that the bride was behind schedule so we were okay on time.

It was time for the wedding to start, and everything went well until it came time for the names.

"Do you, John Jones, take Suzie Cue to be your lawfully wedded wife?" I asked. (No, these were not their actual names.)

The groom looked at me and said, "That is not my name."

I looked at my cheat notes in my Bible.

I thought that maybe I didn't say it correctly. I had taken it right off the marriage license. I repeated myself.

"Do you, John Jones, take Suzie Cue to be your lawfully wedded wife?" I asked again, thinking I said it correctly this time.

John looked at me again and said, "That's not my name!"

I was not feeling well.

I was not getting any help from the groom or the bride.

"What is your name?" I asked, sending the church into fits of laughter.

"My name is John Cue!" he said, frustrated.

I had used her last name as his. Feeling sicker than ever, and embarrassed now as well, I carried on.

"Will you, John Cue, take Suzie Jones to be your lawfully wedded wife?"

He said "I do," and the wedding continued without any more hitches—except the part where they got hitched.

I had mixed up the last names.

I felt like I had ruined the day that the bride wanted to be perfect. I introduced the newly married couple: "Ladies and gentlemen, I present to you Mr. and Mrs. John Cue." They walked out of the chapel to the reception area.

The bride's uncle had asked me to perform the marriage months earlier. When he walked into the reception, I went to him and apologized. I told him that I felt like I destroyed this wonderful day for them. The uncle's response was unexpected.

"Frank, you saved this wedding."

It had nearly been called off. The fact that I had been late in arriving didn't matter. These two families had a major fight over some minor issue that had blown up so much that they nearly canceled the wedding.

"Frank, you broke the ice and allowed angry families to laugh. You actually saved this marriage."

I didn't really believe him, but it provided some solace.

Several months later, I ran into the uncle and his sister, the bride's mother. I, again, apologized for the wedding disaster.

She laughed and said, "You saved the day."

We all laughed.

Names are important.

Names can hurt: "cripple," "loser," "fatty."

I remember in elementary school, my physical education teacher asked me a question as class was starting.

"Are you the smart one or the dumb one?" the teacher asked, referring to my brother and me.

I was taken aback and didn't know how to answer. I didn't think either of us was dumb. I came home sad that day and told my mom what the teacher said. Guess who my mother met with in a private and very serious parent/teacher conference.

We don't accept being called derogatory names.

We would not allow a teacher to use our child's name in a derogatory way.

Each student and each name, hard to pronounce or not, are valued. When it comes to names, you want people to know yours.

You want people to call you by your name.

When you call the mayor's office, you want the mayor's office to know your name.

You want your banker to know your name.

You want your insurance guy to know your name.

You want your preacher to know your name.

In 2003, we asked famed radio broadcaster Paul Harvey to come and speak at a fundraiser for the Community Foundation, of which I was president.

One of my friends told me that a client, a doctor, was friends with Harvey. I told him that I doubted that Harvey knew his client.

My friend wanted to know if he could bring him by the reception to say hello to Harvey.

"Paul Harvey doesn't know your friend," I said doubtfully.

"Yes, he does. They are friends."

I laughed and told my friend that I didn't believe him, but that was a good attempt—such a good attempt that his doctor friend could come and meet Harvey.

The day came for Paul Harvey to come to Jackson.

The reception was packed and was about to end. The attendees left to find their seats for the dinner, then the speech.

Harvey and I were standing around for a bit, eating some of the reception food before going down to start the dinner.

We were about to leave. Harvey looked up and said, "William, it is so good to see you!"

Harvey called Dr. Crook by name.

My friend, Keith, who was with Dr. Crook, looked at me and grinned as he said, "See, I told you that they were friends."

We laughed. As Harvey and Dr. Crook talked, you could tell that they were not just friends, but very good friends.

Can you imagine someone famous knowing your name? Can you imagine a famous person calling out your name from a crowd?

That happened to Zacchaeus.

Jesus walked up to the tree where Zacchaeus had climbed so he could hear Jesus. "Zacchaeus, come down. I want to go home with you and eat dinner."

That dinner with Jesus changed this man's life. Jesus called him by name!

There was a Sunday, an early resurrection morning. Jesus had died and been buried in a borrowed grave. Mary Magdalene had gone to the grave.

The stone was rolled away. Jesus was not in the tomb.

"Woman, why are you weeping?" someone asked her. She thought this was the gardener of the cemetery.

"Sir, if you have taken His body, tell me where you have put it and I will take care of it," she pleaded, not knowing it was Jesus.

"Mary," He called her by her name.

Mary recognized His voice and knew it was Jesus.

Remember the story of Lazarus?

Jesus stood at the grave of Lazarus. This is the story with the shortest verse in the Bible: "Jesus wept."

That story is a tough one.

It involves Mary and Martha's brother. Jesus loved Mary, Martha, and Lazarus.

Jesus had a point to make.

Mary and Martha sent word to Jesus that Lazarus was dying. Instead of going to Bethany, where His three friends lived, Jesus stayed where He was.

It was days later that Jesus told His disciples that they had to go to Bethany, because Lazarus was "asleep." After some discussion, Jesus told them Lazarus had died and they had to go wake him.

Jesus arrived.

Martha came to meet Him: "If only you had been here, Jesus!"

Mary came to meet Him: "Lord, if only you had been here."

They took Jesus to the tomb.

Jesus wept.

The people saw Jesus crying and they understood His love for Lazarus. What they probably didn't understand was that it bothered Jesus that people suffered so that God could show how serious He is about you and me.

I don't believe that Jesus wept because Lazarus had died.

I don't believe Jesus wept because He couldn't get there in time.

I believe Jesus wept because people had to suffer in order for His power to be shown.

Standing at the grave, Jesus called His friend by name.

"Lazarus, come forth."

That day, Jesus's friend walked out of the grave and into the arms of his loved ones. Lazarus would live to die another day.

We know how fathers love calling their children special names.

Princess.

Sweetheart.

Superman.

Terms of endearment.

Special names that show their love.

I remember as a child watching Ira North on TV. He would come to our church when I was a teenager; he was an amazing preacher. Each Sunday, he went and stood by a large book near the baptistry. It was his prayer list. These were people he prayed for daily, and he prayed for them each week on the TV show.

As a kid, I wrote Ira North a letter. I wanted him to know my name, and to put my name in the book with all the others he prayed for. I felt it important that Ira North pray for me.

He added my name and prayed for me daily.

You have a name.

God knows your name.

He knows your heart.

He knows that your imperfections were washed away by grace.

No matter who you are, where you've been, or what you've done, remember: God is love. Perfect love. Your name is in His heart, because He loves you. And His grace is there for you. He has planned a special day for you from before the world was formed, because He loves you.

You are not a mistake. You are His child. You are His heir.

He has had a plan. He carried out that plan so He could enjoy your special day with Him.

Jesus tells of a shepherd.

The shepherd knows his sheep. He calls them by name. They follow him. They even get lost. He leaves the ninety-nine and finds that single lost lamb.

Jesus told that story because you are that important to Him. You are that lamb.

He knows you are not perfect. He knows you will fall. He is there to bring you back into the ninety-nine.

So if you ever feel unworthy, think of others who also felt unworthy:

Think of the woman caught in adultery.

Think of the dishonest tax collector Jesus sought out.

Think of the man of the Gaderenes, the man Jesus traveled all night to reach.

Think of the prodigal son.

Jesus doesn't care about your past. He cares about your heart.

Trust Him to get you through the bad times: the death of a loved one, financial ruin. He can make it better.

Remember that your life is not about today.

This life has pain and hardship.

It has hate and despair.

He wants you to understand that there is coming a day when there are no more heartaches.

No more tears.

No more pain.

We will go to a place that is our home. Our loved ones are there. God has ever so gently transported them there. They are waiting for us.

My friends and family are awaiting my arrival.

I'll see you there.

CHAPTER 6

Love Sees Us Through

Life is never easy. People struggle. Children can be a challenge. Neighbors can be a challenge.

Coworkers can be a challenge. Marriage can be a challenge.

When people, children, neighbors, coworkers, and marriage become difficult, one thing seems to be lacking.

I served as president of a wonderful private Christian school in my hometown.

My parents were so proud of their son being in such a wonderful position, president at a school that was so loved by the community and by the church.

I had "come home."

After three years there, I decided to return to my alma mater to work in fundraising. I am sure my parents had some disappointment that their son was not going to be president of the school they loved, in the city they loved.

I was very young. The job of being president was challenging and stressful.

After three years, I needed to move on. I went to a place where

I felt more capable and could be with my "university family."

One Sunday afternoon not long after I announced my decision, I was with my parents down on their farm. We were out in the front yard drinking iced tea and enjoying the day in the shade of a huge, beautiful tree.

My parents loved me. They had always loved me. I knew that.

However, I grew up in a time when love wasn't often expressed verbally (other than by mothers and grandmothers telling their grandchildren).

Sitting in the shade, we talked about the horses, the cows, the garden, and when the tomatoes would be ripe.

My mother changed the subject abruptly.

She felt the need to get beyond our conversation about cows and horses and tomatoes; we could talk about all that anytime or not at all.

That afternoon, my mom wanted her child, who was leaving our hometown, to hear something so much more important.

She knew the cows and horses were important, but they were going to be fine. The tomatoes were delicious, but they were going to be fine. What Mom did not know was whether her son was going to be fine.

Transition is hard. Leaving is hard.

On that warm Sunday, Mom was about to pour out her heart.

I wasn't just changing jobs, I was moving away.

Away from them.

Away from their protection.

Possibly feeling away from their love.

Mom's words caught me off guard.

"Son, please know that we love you!"

Even Dad was surprised.

"Son, please know that we love you, and you will never do anything that will separate you from our love."

We all got quiet, teary-eyed.

This Middle Tennessee couple who didn't really express emotion that often wanted to make sure it was firmly clear to their oldest son, that he knew the extent of their love.

They wanted their oldest son to know their love would be with him wherever he lived and whatever he did.

I will never forget that day, because this was when I began to have a conscious sense of their commitment to me: unconditional love. That day also gave me a sense of the love that my Heavenly Father has toward His children.

I sleep better at night knowing the love of family and the love of God.

Are your teenage children a challenge?

Overwhelm them with unconditional love.

Are your neighbors a burden and a problem?

Overwhelm them with unconditional love.

Is your marriage troubled?

Overwhelm your spouse with your unconditional love, the same love that brought you together.

Are you troubled by sin in your community?

There is a solution: Love.

Not anger or hate.

Do you think that the future of this country is headed to total destruction?

There is a solution: Love.

Not anger or hate.

There was a time when the Creator became human and left us some guidelines about how to deal with one another: children, coworkers, neighbors, spouses, countries, sinners, people you hate.

When they trouble you, you get to punish them with . . . love.

Love.

"If your enemy is hungry, give him food. In doing this, you will heap burning coals on his head."

"Husbands, love your wives."

"Fathers, do not provoke your children to wrath."
"Love your neighbor as yourself."
"If they compel you to go a mile, go with them two."
"If they strike you on your cheek, turn the other cheek."
Love wins. Love will always win.
If you've read this far, just know I love you . . . *really*!

CHAPTER 7

It's All about Power

George Washington, the father of our country, has inspired generations, but events were not always as portrayed in our children's storybooks.

It was December 25, 1776.

Having suffered defeat after defeat, General Washington made a daring move that changed the future of this nation.

We seem to forget that Washington was not always successful in fighting the British.

Only a few days before Christmas, Washington's army had been chased out of New York. Lord Cornwallis had driven Washington's army across the river, through Pennsylvania, and into New Jersey.

Washington and his troops were in disrepair, totally discouraged. That winter seemed the coldest they could remember.

A remarkable number of Washington's troops died or deserted. Many soldiers had gone home. Those remaining longed for the day when their enlistment was completed. For many, that day was near, so they hung on—but barely.

Even with so many things against him, George Washington didn't give up. He was considering a bold move against the British. That unexpected attack happened on the evening of Christmas Day in 1776. Washington crossed the dangerous, frozen Delaware River.

The crossing had been tried and failed before. Few in Washington's leadership anticipated this time would be a success.

They were facing what might be their last battle. Washington ordered the troops to be prepared for three days of fighting. If they lost, they would go home defeated and face punishment from the British. If they won, this could lead them to victory and freedom.

Around four o'clock that Christmas afternoon, the soldiers learned they were about to take part in a surprise mission. They headed for the river.

Marching eight soldiers abreast, all with new flints and powder, the men crossed the river on large ferry boats. Moving forward under cover of a dark winter night and deathly cold winds, Washington made sure the British would not suspect an attack. Crossing the Delaware River under such severe conditions aided our troops, but also increased the risk for failure.

Washington and his men positioned themselves for the attack. The battle began early December 26, surprising the British troops. Washington's plan worked.

His men defeated the British. He lost only two men, with fewer than ten injured. The British and Hessians lost so much more. The attack took the lives of twenty-two men. Eighty-three soldiers were badly injured.

The battle was won. Washington captured nearly a thousand of the British troops. Washington gained all of the British guns, cannons, and gunpowder.

Washington's daring attack revived the spirit of this new country and energized its patriots' commitment to freedom. Three more critical battles followed. Washington continued to defeat the British. History dubbed him the "father of our country."

Nations pick leaders because of their might and power. Great men of battle are held in high esteem, and people look to them for leadership during difficult times.

Every country dreams of bold new leaders to lead like their forefathers did during past glory days.

There is a period of time between the Old Testament and the New Testament where little is recorded. Israel was controlled by the Seleucid emperor called Antiochus.

Antiochus ruled with an iron fist. He wanted to remove the Jewish religion from the world. It was 167 years before the birth of Christ. With the Seleucid emperor in control of Israel, many Jewish people had lost hope. They longed for the promised Messiah they envisioned as their redeemer. They had been controlled too long, hated by too many. They needed a Washington to come in and save the day.

At that time, there was a Jewish priest named Mattathias. A Seleucid official asked Mattathias to offer a sacrifice in the Temple to one of the Greek gods.

Mattathias refused, but a fellow Jewish man stepped up to make the offering. Mattathias was furious that a fellow Jew would agree to offer a sacrifice to a false god. With his bare hands, Mattathias killed the man. Mattathias then took a sword and killed the governmental representative standing with them.

Evidently, these three were not alone. There was a crowd of witnesses. Mattathias yelled to all those who watched the killings, "Let everyone who has zeal for the law of God and His covenant, follow me!"

With that, Mattathias took his five sons and hundreds of men and led them into the wilderness to form a rather successful resistance to the Seleucid government over the Jewish people.

Mattathias led the revolt only a short time. Before his death, he handed the reins of power to his son, Judas.

Like George Washington, Judas became a leader driven by

passion. He was so resolute that his name became Judas Maccabeus, meaning "Judas the Hammer" from the Aramaic word *maqqaba*, meaning *hammer* or *sledgehammer*.

Judas Maccabeus led Israel against the Seleucid forces after his father's death.

This small but committed group of Jewish men began to fight unconventionally. Judas knew he could not defeat the Seleucid army in a head-to-head battle. He had to catch them off guard. He could win by surprising them.

He could win battles by attacking at night.

He could win by attacking small groups of soldiers.

Eventually, Judas drove the Seleucid army to the sea and away from Israel.

Judas Maccabeus became a hero. Like George Washington, Judas restored hope that many had lost in the fight for God.

So many things changed with Judas Maccabeus after the Seleucids were gone.

It was now time to restore the country, even worship.

On December 14, 164 BC, after the Seleucid defeat, the rededication of the Temple took place. A lamp in the Temple that needed to burn for eight days had enough oil for only one day. The lamp didn't go out.

The first day ended and the lamp continued to burn.

The second day ended . . . and there was the candle still burning. Day after day, the lamp continued to burn.

The lamp burned for the required eight days. It was a miracle that enhanced the story of Judas Maccabeus.

To Israel, Judas became a prototype of the Messiah.

As scripture promised, there would be a Messiah. Judas seemed to fit the bill.

To many, Judas was the one to bring back the glory and the kingdom promised generations earlier. He defeated the Seleucid empire—who but Judas could restore the glory of God's people?

They believed that Judas had the political strength to bring back God's kingdom.

They longed for that promise to be fulfilled in their lifetime, to be restored to the glory of God's kingdom under King David and King Solomon.

That did not happen.

Israel was still looking for that Messiah.

More than two hundred years after Judas Maccabeus, nothing had changed. The people of Israel still longed for the promised one. Others had popped up and made an attempt to be the new Messiah, but it never worked out.

Then someone different came along.

The people saw a new Judas Maccabeus right in their midst. This next guy was a man with potential.

They began to listen to a man who walked quietly but won the hearts of the people.

No one before had spoken like this one did.

He touched hearts but then was able to do miracles. This man named Jesus seemed to be their next new Savior.

In their minds, they saw that Jesus was the new "hammer." Jesus was the one who had the ability to free them from the oversight of Rome, their current oppressor.

It was an understatement that Israel longed for the return of God's kingdom!

When Jesus came into the picture, they thought: *Finally, God is delivering His people out of bondage.*

Jesus, the new King David.

Jesus, the new Judas Maccabeus.

Jesus is the Savior against Rome.

Jesus traveled the countryside preaching about the coming kingdom. That is what they were looking for! Jesus talked their language. The children of Israel began to see Jesus as God's anointed. He fit the mold.

He healed the sick.
He gave sight to the blind.
He raised the dead.

Jesus knew the right words. Jesus said the kingdom was at hand, so Israelites looked to Him as their present-day Judas Maccabeus. They began to think that at some point Jesus would unite the Jewish people and overturn the power that Rome had over them. This is what messiahs do!

Messiahs rescue their people from oppressors.

Even in His hometown, He spoke powerfully—but something was not right. The message was different. They had never expected a Messiah like this.

Jesus commanded them to:

Forgive those who have wronged you.

Pray for those who oppress you.

Love your enemies.

Something did not seem right about this Messiah.

What they had longed for was not what they were finding in Jesus. Surely, when the time came, Jesus would take control, lead an army, and defeat Rome.

Yes! Jesus was saying all these good things about how Jewish people should live at peace. But when the time came, Jesus would take the leadership role and lead a revolutionary army against Rome and free God's people.

"Jesus the Maccabeus!"

"Jesus the Hammer!"

If He was not the Judas of two hundred years earlier, who else could be?

Jesus performed miracles!

Jesus fed the people!

Jesus had thousands to follow Him.

Perhaps the Messiah didn't have to be exactly like Judas Maccabeus.

With Jesus, what they saw was a weak Judas Maccabeus, but He did come with one major plus: miracles.

Going from town to town, Jesus preached, taught, walked, healed, and raised the dead. Judas Maccabeus was not able to do that, but Jesus did!

Yes, Jesus was their Messiah! He had to be!

Jesus gained thousands of followers. They had never followed anyone else like they followed him. Judas Maccabeus didn't have that many followers. Yes, Jesus was their Messiah.

Well, maybe. Something was not quite right.

In His hometown of Nazareth, Jesus was so much the opposite of what they perceived their Messiah should be that they took Jesus out to a cliff and intended to push Him off to His death—but something went wrong.

Jesus disappeared into the angry mob.

Jesus disappeared into the crowd in His hometown, where they were ready to kill Him because He didn't fit the idea of their coming king.

What was happening?

Why was Jesus, the man with miracles, not doing what they needed Him to do to restore the kingdom?

They wanted a kingdom of power! Jesus was definitely not Judas the Hammer. Jesus seemed too weak.

They wanted a kingdom of retribution! Like Judas and his dad, Mattathias. They wanted Rome to suffer defeat and pay for what it had done to Israel.

They wanted a kingdom of vengeance.

Jesus was not that type of king. They wanted all of the glory that they thought was prophesied. What they had was a king of love and forgiveness, the farthest thing from retribution or vengeance. The people of Israel knew that love and forgiveness would not conquer Rome. Love and forgiveness would not free them from the vengeful hand of Herod.

Yet it seems that some of Jesus's closest friends were also expecting the revolt to begin.

In the Garden of Gethsemane, we find Peter with a sword.

Leading an army into Gethsemane, we find a Judas, perhaps to lead the revolt against these men.

Two of the twelve were doing things that were not typical. Doing things not part of their daily ministry.

This Judas was leading an army of men to Jesus.

Did Judas think that the army would kill Jesus? I don't think so. Perhaps Judas thought that Jesus needed help getting the revolt started. He was Judas Iscariot, an embezzler. Judas was greedy.

Perhaps Judas thought, *I am going to help Jesus lead the insurrection against Rome. I get paid for bringing them to Him, greet Him with a kiss, and force Jesus to start the revolution. Jesus will win, and I'm on the winning side with Jesus and a few shekels to the good.*

To Judas, one of the twelve, Jesus was not the same caliber of man as the hammer, Judas Maccabeus. Perhaps Judas lost hope in Jesus, just like the people in Jesus's hometown, because Jesus was not seen as a warrior like their previous heroes.

Jesus had talked every day about the coming kingdom.

Even Jesus's own disciples argued about who would be the greatest in His kingdom.

So many in Jesus's day believed He would become like Judas Maccabeus, fully expecting that Jesus would someday become the king. Even His disciples' parents went to Jesus asking that their sons be on His right and left hand in the new kingdom.

They saw the new kingdom without Rome. They saw Jesus as the new king of Israel.

But something didn't quite fit.

Peter came that day into the Garden of Gethsemane after telling Jesus just a few hours before, "Lord, I will die with you."

Peter saw in Jesus the "hope of Israel" that had been prophesied.

At the Last Supper, Peter so strongly believed that Jesus would become the new "hammer" that he said, "Lord, I will never deny you." Peter had been with Jesus for three years and knew that no one could do what Jesus did!

Peter believed with all his heart that Jesus would someday soon become the new king of Israel.

Peter believed that Jesus would become his present-day Judas the Hammer.

What transpired that night after the Garden of Gethsemane made Peter question everything he had previously believed.

Peter saw his hopes of Jesus being the new king dashed at the cross.

Peter, like many others, looked for a strong leader to take their country back.

When you are human—even when you have experienced miraculous, unbelievable events—it is so hard to wrap your brain around something other than a physical kingdom.

According to prophesy, the glory of David and Solomon's kingdom would be restored.

What Peter experienced in Gethsemane was nothing like what their ministers and teachers had been preaching in the synagogues.

Men came at Jesus with swords and spears.

What did Peter do? He grabbed his sword! Peter was like so many of us!

Sometimes God's presence in our daily lives doesn't fit with how we imagine or expect it to be.

"Lord, I'll die with you!"

I know you are the Messiah! Peter was probably thinking. *You are our Judas Maccabeus! I will fight with you as we bring back GOD'S KINGDOM!*

Then that didn't happen.

The Messiah didn't appear as expected.

Peter put everything he had into Jesus being the Messiah . . . the Judas Maccabeus . . . Jesus the Hammer.

When the army approached Jesus, Peter picked up the sword

to begin the revolution—and cut someone's ear off.

Jesus the Maccabeus told Peter to put down the sword.

Peter thought he was beginning the battle. Peter thought he was helping Jesus to start the revolution.

"Peter, put down the sword," Jesus said. He picked up the ear of Malchus, the high priest's servant, and put it back on.

Jesus as a "Judas Maccabeus" disappointed Peter.

Then Jesus was taken away. The revolution did not start. Jesus was in the hands of Rome, the enemy! This is not what Peter was expecting. Jesus could not be what God had planned.

Lost and confused, Peter was trying to figure out where he went wrong. *How could I put so much faith in this man to return the glory to God's kingdom and be so disappointed?*

Peter followed them at a distance and was confronted: "This man was with Jesus."

"I do not know him."

Again he was confronted: "You are one of them."

"I am not!"

And again: "Sir, I do not know the man!"

Peter honestly did not know this man who was now before Pilate. He expected a different man at this point; he expected an insurrection. He got a Messiah standing before the Roman ruler facing a public execution.

Who is this man who convinced me that He was the Messiah? How could I have fallen for someone who fell so short of what I believed the Messiah would be?

"I DO NOT KNOW THE MAN!"

At this point, Peter was totally lost as to whom Jesus was.

Nothing seemed as it should be.

"I DO NOT KNOW THE MAN!"

Jesus was not what anyone had expected.

There have been times in my life when God didn't fit the idea that I had.

I expected God to behave a certain way, and He didn't.

At this writing, there is a child dealing with life-threatening cancer, and God allows this innocent child to suffer.

A friend's husband, at the peak of his medical career, was struck by a car and killed. He was a godly father, husband, and friend.

A couple of bad guys fighting it out with guns sent a bullet through the air, striking a child. An innocent child was killed and the killers got away.

The love of your life is taken from you.

My friend's child drowns in a boating accident.

Life is not what you expected, and God allows it to happen.

Just like Peter. Just like the people of Jesus's hometown. There are times that God doesn't fit the mold that I expected.

I expected vengeance.

I expected retribution.

I expected paybacks.

Jesus talks about love, and we don't understand.

We want someone to pay for the hurt we have experienced—and Jesus tells us to love.

Why can't He be "Jesus Maccabeus"?

Why can't Jesus run this world fairly?

Why? Why? Why?

Jesus only says to love.

We want "Judas the Hammer" verses "Jesus the Lamb."

To us, it just doesn't make sense. It didn't make sense to those in Jesus's day, either—payback versus forgiveness and love.

In a world that celebrates vengeance, Jesus didn't fit.

World wars start because of paybacks.

Politics becomes dirty because of paybacks.

Divorces become mean because of paybacks.

Revenge is not sweet.

I don't know the answers, but I do know that Jesus said to love. Love our enemies. Love those who hate us.

Jesus talks about the kingdom and we do not comprehend it. We want Judas Maccabeus and power in the physical world. We struggle to understand the kingdom of God, a spiritual kingdom.

When Lazarus was deathly sick, something odd happened.

Jesus waited. Jesus loved Lazarus, but He waited four days to head for Lazarus's hometown.

Lazarus suffered. Family members struggled. Jesus was a no-show. Lazarus died. The funeral was huge. The city turned out for the funeral and then they went to be with the family.

Then Jesus came to town.

That day, Jesus cried.

That day, Jesus came to town to raise Lazarus from the dead.

That day, God showed the world that Jesus, the Messiah, had power over death—at the expense of Lazarus and his family.

That day, it hurt God to see humans hurting.

I don't know what the long-term goal is when it comes to suffering. I do know that when people hurt, God hurts.

I do not understand the things of this world that hurt people.

I do understand that God loves His people, and His people are not perfect.

His people are caught in adultery.

Living in cemeteries.

Have dreaded diseases.

Are prodigal sons.

And He welcomes us all home to be with Him, even though we do not deserve it.

I don't quite get it, when He says to love. Love doesn't fit how I see God working.

I understand that this world is not my home. This world is controlled by darkness.

No matter who I am, what I have done, where I have been, I am God's child and He wants me home with him. That home is not here.

My friend, the kingdom of Heaven is still at hand. Let me trust Jesus with this.

God is love.

Love your neighbor as yourself.

Love God with all your heart.

We'll be fine, because *He* is good.

*"You are the most expensive thing ever created.
You cost the Father everything to have you with Him."*

CHAPTER 8

The President Came to Town

I was young. This happened while I went to Highland Park Elementary School in Columbia.

It was 1967, and my hometown was the first city in the state to have a community college. That was a big enough deal to bring in the president of the United States!

It was Mom and me. I don't know where my brother was. Mom thought this was important enough for her to bring a son to watch the president come to town.

We stood in front of the Presbyterian church in downtown Columbia. It was a gray day. Not raining, but gray. We stood and stood. I don't remember having a conversation. We just stood on the curb of West Seventh Street to see the president.

We were not alone. All along West Seventh Street, people were standing. Waiting for the president.

Right beside us was a former president's home—James K. Polk—but he was president a long time ago. Polk's home was not as big as other presidents' homes. It is kind of simple, but elegant.

It wasn't too long before people began to get excited. Police cars with sirens and flashing lights came down the street. A long line of cars led the way after the police cars.

Then there was the president's long, black car.

We watched it come closer and closer, then it was right in front of us, then we watched as it continued out of sight.

I saw the president: Lyndon Baines Johnson.

Technically, I didn't see the president. I did see a figure I assumed was the president in the back seat of the car.

There was a time when presidents rode in uncovered cars.

President John F. Kennedy rode in an uncovered car. He was shot while riding in that kind of car. The people along the streets in Dallas could see President Kennedy. I didn't actually get to see President Johnson for that reason.

Johnson became president because Kennedy was shot.

That shooting shocked this country.

That shooting changed this country.

I remember days of coverage on our little black-and-white TV after John F. Kennedy was shot. It was a sad time in America.

But, when President Johnson came to Columbia, it was a big day, a fun day, an exciting day!

An interesting thing happened when President Johnson was leaving town. The line of cars came down West Seventh Street just like when they came in. They turned onto North Garden Street, to take the president to the airport in Nashville.

This great line of cars was carrying the most important person in the world, the leader of the free world. No power known to man was going to be able to stop his trip from Columbia to Nashville.

But then, there was this.

Evidently the leader of the free world was looking out the window of his limousine and saw a Dairy Queen. The long line of police cars, highway patrol cars, and Secret Service cars . . . *stopped*.

Someone from the president's limousine jumped out and ran into Dairy Queen. The president's car stood still in the middle of

North Garden Street. Traffic all over downtown Columbia came to a stop. Nothing moved until the guy from the president's car came out of Dairy Queen with milkshakes and jumped into the presidential limousine.

Columbia was happy that the president came. This grade-school kid was happy that day because he got to see the president, even if he didn't get to see the president. The president was happy that he got milkshakes from Dairy Queen.

It didn't take much to make us happy back in the day.

Having the president in town was a big deal.

That was probably a political move by the president, the governor, and the mayor. Our town was happy. Surely the governor and our mayor were happy.

Maybe that was statesmanship. Maybe it was politics. Those two concepts are totally different.

I have friends who are politicians. They do government stuff. Perhaps good stuff. They are always working on political deals with other politicians.

I have known a statesman or two. They lead. They are rare. They are not politicians.

Our country longs for statesmen. We really, really, *really* would rather have statesmen and not politicians.

There was a time when James and John, the sons of Zebedee, became like politicians.

"Lord, will you grant us our request, whatever we ask?"

"What is your request?" Jesus asked.

"Lord, will you allow us to sit on your left and your right when you come into your kingdom?"

"Wow! Both of you want to be at my side when I come into my kingdom?"

"Yes! We are two of your closest friends in our group. Well, there is the other John. But besides John, we are probably your two closest friends among your disciples. We want to be your right hand and your left. We need thrones on each side of yours."

"Well, let me think."

James and John were from Bethsaida. They were fishermen.

Jesus called James and John to follow him. They did. Right after they left their nets and were among the disciples, Jesus renamed them. They became the "Sons of Thunder."

When the Creator of the world renames you "Sons of Thunder," do you think they were loud?

Do you think they created a storm at times?

Do you think they were full of themselves?

There were probably some things about these two that were not quiet or calm. They were probably loud, forceful, and ambitious.

They took a trip to Jerusalem. Little did James and John know, this would be the last trip to Jerusalem with Jesus.

James and John, along with Peter, Judas, Andrew, Philip, Thomas, Matthew, and others knew that Jesus was the Messiah. They realized that Jesus was the Messiah a long time ago.

They saw Jesus raise the dead, feed thousands, heal the sick, and confound the Pharisees, Sadducees, Zealots, and religious leaders. They knew about religious leaders—like Nicodemus, who came to Jesus by night to ask questions—because some of the religious leaders believed that Jesus was the Messiah.

Being the Messiah brought expectations. Big ones.

The Messiah was a David kind of guy. King David was the expectation given by scripture. The Messiah would be great like triumphal King David.

David killed Goliath. David won battles. David built a country. After David, King Solomon was great and the kingdom was grand. Solomon brought wealth and power to the kingdom of Israel.

Israel expected that the Messiah would bring all that glory back to Israel.

After Solomon, the kingdom began a downward spiral. Maybe there was a good king at times, but there were also very bad kings.

People longed for the prophesied Messiah who would restore the kingdom of David.

You may remember how things got complicated at the end of David's life.

Absalom set a field on fire, attempted a coup, and was killed. Solomon became king.

Later, Israel became divided into two groups, two kings.

Prophets were sent. Never good news.

Well, Isaiah had good news. The others, not so much.

Life was not good.

Both countries, Israel and Judah (the two countries that used to be one), were sent into captivity about seven hundred years before Christ.

The Old Testament ends. Then we see something start to happen. There is this period of time between the Old Testament and the New Testament.

While living in captivity in Israel, a priest named Mattathias called on God to bring His people out of captivity. He led a revolt that began to turn the tide against their oppressors.

On his deathbed, Mattathias urged his children to be zealous for the law and to remember the deeds of their ancestors.

"Gather about you all who observe the law, and avenge your people," he advised them.

After Mattathias died, his son Judas rose up and became a powerful Zealot. Many thought that Judas was the messiah who God would send to save His people. Many of the men of Israel at that time saw Judas Maccabeus as their messiah.

Judas and his father began a group that later became the Zealots of Jesus's day, quietly trying to overthrow the government of Rome.

Judas fit the role they expected of a messiah. Strong. Powerful. Evidently he looked like a messiah. The people looked to him for hope and freedom.

Judas Maccabeus wanted to bring Israel out of captivity and return it to God.

Israel saw Judas Maccabeus as a strong leader who could re-establish God's kingdom in Jerusalem.

Israel rallied behind Judas as he tried to overthrow the government. He and his men began a guerilla war to bring back David's kingdom, an earthly kingdom.

Judas became a political leader in the eyes of Israel, much like our George Washington.

James and John, just like Judas Maccabeus, expected an earthly kingdom. They asked to have thrones on each side of Jesus's throne as He ruled. They believed Jesus would lead them out of the captivity of Rome.

James and John. Peter and Judas. Matthew and Philip. All of the twelve fully expected Jesus to become the ruler of Israel, just like David. They expected Jesus would become the king of Israel by the power of God. They were on their way to Jerusalem to help Jesus become king. Anticipating an uprising, James and John approached Jesus to make their request.

"Teacher, we want you to do for us whatever we ask."

What they meant was:

1. We want to sit with you,
2. In your glory,
3. One on your right,
4. One on your left,
5. Enthroned,
6. Sharing royal power with Jesus.

"You do not know what you are asking. You are not able to endure what you are asking," He must have told them.

"We can," they said.

We are the Sons of Thunder! You chose us! You named us! You know us! You have seen and heard us! We are capable leaders to rule with you!

Jesus knew He was just miles from Gethsemane and days from Golgotha. His two friends did not.

"James and John, you will drink from the bitter cup and will be baptized with the suffering that is about to come. But I cannot grant who is on my left and right. God has chosen those."

They were asking for something they didn't understand about this kingdom.

Even the devil didn't understand what Jesus was talking about. The devil took Jesus on a high mountain and showed Him all the kingdoms of the world.

Satan told Jesus: "These kingdoms and their glory have all been given to me. I can give it to whomever I will. I will give it to you; all the kingdoms of the world will be yours."

James and John had that same idea of glory in an earthly kingdom.

Patriotism brings pride and wars and death and more death. Glory of conquest. Wars won. The glory of being triumphant over your enemy. The glory of parades recognizing conquest. James and John were seduced by that.

The glory of God is not a story of conquest but of redeeming love. Everlasting love. Unearned love.

Kingdoms are not typically run with love but with power. The kingdom of God doesn't make sense, because it is not an earthly kingdom. The love of God, while not always visibly apparent, was even in the Old Testament.

The Old Testament seemed to be only about sacrifice and rules: "Take a lamb, without spot, without blemish." The Holy of Holies. The Most Holy Place. The room beyond the curtain where the Mercy Seat sat on top of the Ark of the Covenant. For generations, sacrifices were made for the people.

The whole concept of scripture was about a sacrifice—a sacrifice that James and John didn't quite understand.

They didn't have the perspective of hindsight. The priests and

Pharisees did not understand. They were living in the moment. The disciples did not understand yet.

Jesus was on His way to become the sacrificial lamb, not take control of power.

Jesus was the lamb "without spot or blemish."

James and John, like all Israelites, expected an earthly kingdom. They were used to offering sacrifices. This last trip to Jerusalem, to James and John, was about taking control in Jerusalem. To Jesus, it was about a sacrifice—His sacrifice.

God had planned this trip to be about a sacrifice, but not of bulls and goats. God had planned the perfect sacrifice that would end animal sacrifices.

A prophesied sacrifice. An expensive sacrifice.

Once upon a time, I bought a red sports car.

I loved that car. It was only a two-seater. It sat low to the ground. It had speakers in the headrests and lights that popped up from the front of the car. It went fast. Too fast.

Friends with raggedy old cars wanted to borrow my shiny red car to take on dates. Cars impress people. They wanted to use my red sports car to impress their date, when evidently they could not impress their date with their personality.

I never let anyone drive that car. I didn't even let my good friends drive it.

Why? I spent everything I had to buy that car. To me, it was a dream car. It was a car that cost me way too much money.

I paid too much money to let one of my friends wreck my car trying to impress some girl whom they could impress without the car. That car was too expensive.

One of my best friends in Florida drives a $250,000 car. He started young and worked hard. He built several businesses. He started with nothing and now has a beautiful home, a yacht, and a couple of expensive cars.

I was visiting him for a little vacation. After dinner, he let me drive his extremely expensive car to his house. I was nervous. It was a beautiful car. I was afraid I would wreck it or scratch it, or break it!

My wonderful friend has worked so hard and raised a wonderful family, but it took sacrifice.

Golgotha is a hill in Jerusalem.

I visited there.

Golgotha is not big.

Golgotha is not pretty.

Golgotha had a road on top of it and a parking lot beneath.

Golgotha didn't have any valuable assets.

Golgotha was about to become the most expensive property on the earth.

The mystery of the cross.

Golgotha was going to become the new Holy of Holies . . . the new Mercy Seat.

The mystery of the cross.

That small hill had a cost that could only be paid by the Creator, with His life.

The mystery of the cross.

Why would God work through such a mystery?

It's the mystery of the cross.

Even a mystery where God chose thugs and robbers to be on His left and His right.

It's the mystery of the cross.

When Rome meant the cross to be a place of shame, Jesus turned it into His glory.

It's the mystery of the cross.

Part of the mystery: God chose men of shame to join Jesus on that day. A convicted thief was escorted into glory.

The mystery of the cross became the glory of the cross.

The kingdom would come through a cross.

Not by bullets or battles.

Not by greed or glory.

Not by winning an election or a war.

The mystery of the cross became a perfect example of love and sacrifice.

Our commandment is to be a community of love.

Our instructions were simple: Love your neighbor.

Our future is to join in a heavenly choir in singing, "Worthy is the Lamb," the only one who could pay that price as the "lamb without spot or blemish."

So as we gather, even with two or three, He has promised to be there, and we remember.

It's just a cracker and some grape juice . . . well, not really.

And we remember.

"This is my body."

"This is my blood."

We remember that it was *that* blood and *that* body, which took a guilty thief into Heaven.

"You proclaim the Lord's death until He returns."

That perfect sacrifice.

In the midst of our imperfections, He says: "There I am in the midst of you."

That cross took God from the Holy of Holies where only the high priest could enter to where now, a group of two brings God into your midst.

"Frank, this story is really kind of preachy."

That is not the intent. The intent is to show that this story is one about value, great value.

You are the most expensive thing in all of creation.

The kingdom of Heaven is like unto a pearl of great price.

The kingdom of Heaven is like unto a treasure found in a field.

I have a friend who was near death. A unique condition damaged his heart beyond repair. Richard was facing death, and he knew it. His beloved wife knew it.

Heart issues changed the dynamics of their family.

Life became more precious. It became intensely precious to Richard and Jan.

A young man on the other side of the country lost his life in an accident. Richard received the word that there was now a heart. There was hope.

The young man's heart was rushed to Tennessee.

My friend was rushed to the hospital.

The process began. In the operating room was this young man's heart, not beating.

They stopped my friend's heart from beating and removed it.

Now both hearts were not beating.

The young man's heart was placed into my friend's body and then came the challenge.

Would the new heart in Richard's body start again?

It did . . . and it kept on beating.

At the time, I had never met a person who had a heart transplant. My friend had never met a person with a heart transplant. Now he is one.

Eventually the young man's family reached out to meet the person who kept their son's heart beating. Their son lives on through my friend.

What an expensive price for life. One life was saved by the loss of another.

You are the most expensive thing ever created.

You cost the Father everything to have you with Him.

The story of the prodigal son is nothing more than a story about the Creator, the Father waiting for you to come back home.

He simply wants His children home, like every father.

He wants every child home. The Father won't let just anything happen to you because you came at a precious price.

The most expensive thing in the world is love.

All that is ever asked of you is to love.

Yes, you are asked only to love.
It will change your world.
It will change *the* world.
It will change you.

CHAPTER 9

Neighbors

We were just kids, maybe eight or nine years old. Dad trained Tennessee walking horses, and I helped out here and there. Usually I was with my brother Mike and my friend Howard, whose dad worked with the horses.

That young, "working" at your dad's horse barn meant there were jobs you couldn't do and jobs you had to do, and did.

We fed and watered the horses and raked the hall.

We were not allowed to:

• Play in the feed room (even though we did).

• Ride on the walker (even though we did). This equipment cooled the horses by walking them in circles after their workout. Kids could jump on it and go around like a carousel.

• Play in the hay lofts above the horses (even though we did).

Beyond that, we were free to go, until we had to go back to "work" at the end of the day.

Our work came at the beginning or at the end of the work day. When we finished morning chores, we did what we loved. We could go exploring on the farm and then climb fences to continue our adventures at someone else's farm. Exploring never ended.

There were ponds that needed rocks skipped on them.

Fences that needed to be climbed over.

Graveyards that needed to be checked out.

Creeks needed to be walked in.

Trees needed to be climbed.

Hay lofts needed to be played in.

With acres and acres to roam, three young boys were in Heaven. Sometimes we would take random horses that were not in training and ride all over the farm. Howard rode a big horse. Mike rode a Shetland pony. I had a Quarter pony.

There were few limitations on the farm. Off we'd go.

Then came lunch. We would head to the barn for lunch. We had limited eating options: Beanee Weenee, hoop cheese, Coke, and MoonPies.

But one day, something special happened.

Rarely did everyone go eat at a restaurant, but this day we were celebrating. I don't remember why, but it had to be significant because it caused us to load up every working person in the barn to go eat. We filled the pickup truck's cab and bed, and a car or two. We drove to the little town of Spring Hill, Tennessee, and pulled into the parking lot of Stan's Restaurant. Everyone loved Stan's. Stan's had mini-jukeboxes on the table and a pinball machine.

Pinball machines were sinful, from what we were told. It was all that "gambling" you did with pinball.

Hummm . . . I never knew of anyone gambling with a pinball machine, but evidently there were people who did. And all that gambling was going to send us to hell.

I think we'd even go to hell if we played one.

I guess it was on the par with face cards.

According to my grandparents, we were going to hell for playing with those also.

They also told me that Elvis was destroying music. I don't

know if listening to Elvis would send you to hell, but they told me how Elvis had destroyed:

Morality.

Music.

Homes.

And lives.

But back to Stan's. Even with that pinball machine in the dining room, the place was always full.

We pulled up in the parking lot, and we all jumped out of the bed and the cab of the pickup and emptied all the cars.

There were probably eight or nine of us in the truck. I don't know about the cars, but we always rode in the back of the pickup. I grabbed my friend Howard, and we started following my dad toward the front door.

Dad looked around and saw us behind him.

"Howard can't eat up here," he said.

Howard and I headed to the back with Howard's dad, Bo.

"Son, come on up here. You can't go back there."

"Why can't I eat with Howard?"

"You just can't."

"Why can't Howard eat with us?"

"Son, Howard just can't eat with us."

I looked around. Howard's dad, Bo, and a couple more folks who worked as grooms were headed to the back door of the restaurant. Bo never questioned where to go. None of the grooms walked to the front of the restaurant.

Howard joined his dad; my dad made sure where I ate.

I ate up front, played the small jukebox on the table, and didn't touch the pinball machine.

When it was time to go, I ran to the back to see where Howard ate. No jukebox. No pinball machine. No booths to eat in, just tables and chairs with people eating out of white paper sacks.

Everyone there was black. There was not a white person in the room except this nine-year-old kid poking his head in the door. Then it hit me: There wasn't a black person in the front part of the restaurant.

It didn't make sense to a nine-year-old.

Exclusion.

A man from Ethiopia was leaving Jerusalem.

He was born in an exclusive family, but was not born Jewish. He had become a Jewish follower and traveled all the way from Ethiopia to Jerusalem to worship.

When you think about it, he was amazing. We are told that he was part of the Ethiopian government. He was the treasurer of the country.

Ethiopia was different from most countries. It was run by women—black women. They had a female monarch. It was during the Kandake (pronounced *Can-dake-key*) reign.

We usually think that monarchs are primarily male.

With a female regent, the men in her service were required to be eunuchs, as was this national treasurer.

So we have a black man, a eunuch, riding a thousand or more miles to worship at the Temple in Jerusalem.

What is wrong with this picture?

This man rode in a chariot for more than a thousand miles—only to learn that according to the first five books of the Bible (the Torah), he could not worship in the Temple.

Imagine how long this trip took.

The treasurer of Ethiopia, his security guards, the servants who provided his meals and supplies for such a long trip. They may have been believers also. This entourage arrived in Jerusalem with one purpose: to worship in the Jewish Temple. He got cleaned up and presentable and headed to the Holy Place. Walking up to the Temple, the treasurer of Ethiopia discovered that he was forbidden to worship there. He may have been important in Ethiopia, but not in the Temple. He was excluded.

He was restricted for two reasons. He was not Jewish, and he was a eunuch. Eunuchs were specifically denied entry to the Temple in Deuteronomy 23.

Exclusion.

Moses wrote Deuteronomy, a book of exclusion, about fifteen hundred years before Christ.

Moses wrote and established the Jewish laws as Israelites left Egypt. These first five books of the Old Testament (the Torah) were about exclusion.

Then there was Isaiah.

Five hundred years before the eunuch's story began, the prophet Isaiah wrote about a future kingdom of *inclusion*.

Isaiah's kingdom was very different from Moses.

Moses, exclusion. Isaiah, inclusion.

Isaiah's prophecy would change the life of that Ethiopian eunuch. After he left Jerusalem, he headed down a desert road toward the town of Gaza.

He was reading a scroll; on it was the Book of Isaiah. This would be an expensive purchase. The Book of Isaiah is not small, and it was transcribed by hand. Meticulously.

Meanwhile, an angel of the Lord spoke to Philip: Go encounter a man in a chariot, reading a scroll from the Book of Isaiah. Philip found him and did just that.

Understand this. The Ethiopian was leaving Jerusalem, disappointed and feeling excluded. As he traveled, he was reading aloud. That's how they read back then. If you could not read, you listened to someone else read and that is how you learned. As he was traveling, a man started to run alongside the chariot. The Ethiopian continued reading from Isaiah: "He was led like sheep to the slaughter . . ."

Philip, beside the chariot, heard him and asked, "Do you understand what you are reading?"

Shortly thereafter, Philip was in the chariot talking about Jesus.

The eunuch had been reading about the kingdom that Jesus established. This kingdom allows foreigners, Moabites, Egyptians, people born illegitimately, and even eunuchs. This kingdom includes everyone.

EVERYONE!

Perhaps this is when it sank in and made sense. Imagine how he must have felt: *Even I—a eunuch, a foreigner—can be part of the kingdom, and acceptable to God?*

As they traveled, they came up to a pool of water.

"Here is water . . ."

They kept me, a foreigner, out of the Temple, he may have thought.

"Here is water . . ."

They kept me, a eunuch, out of the Temple.

"Here is water . . ."

"What restrictions are there that keep me from becoming part of this kingdom?"

Philip looked at the Ethiopian and said, "Do you believe all of this I have told you that was prophesied more than five hundred years ago about Jesus?"

"I do."

"Well, there is nothing that can stop you from being baptized."

"Stop the chariot!"

The Ethiopian came down from the chariot. Philip baptized him. The Ethiopian went on his way, rejoicing.

Inclusion.

A few years ago, I changed churches.

There were many reasons, all important to me.

The first Sunday I visited Skyline, my new church, the minister said something that struck me as odd. Not odd in that it was out of character, I just had not heard it in church, in any church.

"Whoever you are, wherever you have been, whatever you have done . . . you are welcome here."

I had never heard that before. It got my attention. It made me listen more closely to everything that was said or sung. I listened to every song, every word the speakers said that day.

I left the church building that day not believing what I had experienced was real.

I told myself this was too good. This could not be real. I told myself I would never come back because it had to be fake. It seemed like they really wanted people—normal, regular people and not-so-normal or regular people.

All week long, the message of inclusion would not leave my mind. *No church ever says that,* I thought.

The next Sunday, I visited another church, but the message at that Skyline church would not leave my mind.

I came back. The minister got up and spoke to start the service, again saying: "Whoever you are, wherever you've been, whatever you have done . . . you are welcome here!"

Inclusion.

Maybe these people believe this stuff, I thought.

I came back every Sunday.

It took me a little while, but eventually I went to see a friend who was divorced—and excluded—from his church.

"You need to come check out this church."

Then to another divorced friend: "You need to come check out this church!"

They did.

Two families, previously excluded, now felt . . . inclusion.

Jesus told some hated tax collectors, "Come follow me."

Jesus told highly hated, political Zealots, "Come follow me."

Tax collectors worked for the Roman government.

The Zealots were religious extremists trying to remove Roman rule from Israel, even if it involved taking human lives.

Jesus brought together the extremists, and the Samaritans, and the adulterers, and those who denied Him, and even those who were involved in the stoning of Christians.

Inclusion.

The whole concept of such unity is contrary to humanity.

The Roman world was not about inclusion. The notion of a slave being equal with a senator was beyond Rome's ability to grasp.

The Jewish world was not about inclusion. The Temple and all of its glory were about excluding a long list of people, those listed in Deuteronomy 23 and in other places.

The Zealots excluded all those who were not Jewish. They wanted to remove all of Rome from Jewish culture, even if it had to happen by killing.

When the prophets Ezra and Nehemiah preached to Judah and Israel, it was about exclusion.

Yet when Isaiah talked to Judah and Israel about the future kingdom, it was about inclusion.

In AD 50, when the church was so young, no other group on the face of the earth ever talked about inclusion.

To most countries of the world, inclusion was problematic.

Only a small group of people from Jerusalem believed in the notion. Even this small group, called "the church," had difficulty living up to the idea.

Paul had to help them.

The Lord's Supper was celebrated as a dinner. You brought your own. Some were extravagant, even including alcohol. The poor had nothing, sitting near the wealthy with their abundance. Excluded, while celebrating the Lord's death and sacrifice.

Paul had to pay them a visit to help them understand that the Lord's Supper was not about exclusion. The Lord's Supper was not only for those with social standing. It was not about the haves and the have-nots. It was about inclusion.

Simon (Peter) the Zealot and Matthew (Levi) the tax collector—total opposites—began to understand inclusion.

So did the woman at the well, who had five husbands, and Mary Magdalene, whose seven demons were cast out.

Saul—who was involved in stoning the first Christian martyr Stephen—became Paul, the preacher who reminded the world . . .

There is no Jew or Gentile.

There is no slave or free.

There is no male or female.

They were all one in Christ. Inclusion!

The church is all about inclusion.

The entire message of Jesus Christ is about inclusion.

The fact is that Jesus died for:

The destitute,

The school teacher,

The inmate,

The Boy Scout leader

The tattooed,

The Sunday school teacher,

The bar worker,

The garbage collector,

The preacher.

They all become one.

Whom do you include?

Do they live at a certain elevated lifestyle? Drive a certain kind of car? Live in a certain type of house? Do a certain type of work?

As a believer in God, whom do you *not* include?

Are there people you don't want to include? Do they have a D or R by their name? Are they trying to get across the border or over a wall? Is their worship different from yours?

The ultimate test of your Christianity is not in doctrine, but in love. Someone once said it this way:

> *Though I am eloquent so that my words may move men and even angels . . . And if I do not have love in my heart for all men, I am like someone singing off key. And though I give all of my possessions so that poor people can have a place to live*

and food to eat, and though I have the highest understanding of earthly knowledge, and even am able to speak in some heavenly language, love enables me to overlook someone else's shortcomings. Love enables me to be kind to those I might otherwise hold in disdain. Love keeps me from thinking that I am great, when I need to consider myself to be a servant. Love prevents me from taking advantage of people, especially the vulnerable. Love prevents me from wishing ill on another, even though they wish me ill. Love allows me to treat the mean in a kind way.

Dr. Martin Luther King Jr.'s words on his last Christmas Eve to those fighting his efforts of inclusion were:

"We shall match your capacity to inflict suffering by our capacity to endure suffering. We will meet your physical force with our soul force. Do what you want to us, and we will still love you. Be assured that we will wear you down. We will appeal to your heart and conscience, that we will win you in the process."

That doesn't make sense.
Nor does Jesus: "Turn the other cheek."
Nor does Paul: "Love never fails."
Oh, how hard it is to control our tongue and to love those who do not love us.
Ask Stephen. He prayed for his murderers.
Ask Paul. God had to show him a vision to include things previously excluded.
Ask John, whom Jesus loved.
Ask Peter. After breakfast on the beach with Jesus, he had to answer Jesus's question, "Do you love me?"
We live in a time when our country is deeply divided.

There is great animosity toward the other side, but this is not the first time. Our country has been divided before. Politicians seem to have always lacked the ability to see justice.

Even religious leaders excluded people: groups, sinners, different-looking people.

Jesus said, "Come unto me. All of you who are weary. All of you who are heavy laden."

Jesus said *all*.

As the Lord's church and His people, we should be people of inclusion.

"Whoever you are, wherever you have been, whatever you have done . . . you are welcome here!"

*"Jesus asked only the sinless
to throw stones.
It's not your job to yell,
to hate, to throw stones."*

CHAPTER 10

Hold onto Them Tightly

Jerrod was your typical-looking middle school kid who had just moved to town.

He didn't pick the town, the school, or his parents. There were times he didn't want to be involved with any of them, but that is life.

We have all been there. We lived through it with perhaps a few scars. Most guys were the same in middle school. Skinny. Quirky. Shy. Trying to figure everything out. That's not easy for a kid.

Then there is gym. That's never comfortable for a skinny, quirky, shy kid trying to figure out life.

A group of kids this age always has a leader, and it tends to be one who's loud and cruel. Adapting to that pack mentality is rough for anyone not in a clique, and Jerrod didn't have many friends to rely on.

During gym, he didn't do anything that put him into a place of honor or respect. He felt uncomfortable and out of place.

In the dressing room, guys singled him out because he was small. Someone pulled down his shorts and popped him with a towel. Everyone laughed at Jerrod.

It went further. Someone looked at his small frame and called him gay. Everyone laughed.

A couple of guys pushed him into the showers naked. Everyone laughed. Jerrod retreated to a corner of the shower, trying to get away from everyone.

One of the leaders called him derogatory names. Everyone laughed. Another of the leaders began to urinate on Jerrod. Everyone laughed. Someone yelled that they were going to be late to class, so everyone quickly got dressed and left gym class laughing about what all had just happened.

Jerrod realized that everyone had left, turned on the shower, washed the urine off his body, and got dressed. Jerrod gained a sense of composure. He grabbed his books, then walked out of the gym, down the hallway, and out of the school. He walked all the way home. Jerrod went to his bedroom and crashed.

Jerrod was different.

From the gym to his house, Jerrod was a changed person.

He didn't cry.

He didn't smile.

He just walked.

From his bedroom, Jerrod walked to his parents' bedroom and took the gun from the nightstand and walked to the garage.

This was not what Jerrod's parents had envisioned for his life.

This was not how Jerrod pictured his life.

Meanwhile, the school had called Jerrod's mother to let her know he had left without permission.

Frantically, Jerrod's mother went home, trying to find her boy.

She arrived at their home, hoping Jerrod was inside. He was.

Her son was in the garage, alone, lying on an old shower curtain so he would not make a mess.

Suicide is real. Suicide is difficult.

There are so many people who feel like they are emotionally, physically, spiritually, mentally, figuratively . . . lost.

Standing on the edge about to jump.

Everywhere you look, there are people going through hard times, dark times, loveless times. They are losing hope.

In the midst of crowds of people, they are there on the edge of life about to jump. I just want to implore you: If you see someone on the edge . . . GRAB THEM.

Use both hands.

Grab an arm.

Grab a hand.

Grab a leg.

Grab anything you can reach.

Do it through a meal, or a phone call, or a letter, or a Facebook message, or a love offering, or a smile, or a hug. It doesn't matter how you do it. Let the Holy Spirit lead.

But please reach out and grab them!

Grab them so they know that someone, somewhere, cares enough to hold them tight . . . never letting go.

Grab them because you are the hands and arms of Jesus on this earth.

Grab them because there is nothing Jesus wants more than for His people to wrap arms around one another. Hold them tight.

Jesus asked only the sinless to throw stones.

It's not your job to yell, to hate, to throw stones.

So, grab them!

Let Jesus grab them, as you hold them.

Hold on with all your heart.

They may lack faith.

They may be spiritually thirsty.

They may be the woman at the well.

They may be crippled by addictions.

They may be the cripple beside the road.

They may be second-class citizens.

They may be the prodigal son.

They may be gay and rejected by "Christians."
They may be the man of the Gadarenes, living in the cemetery.
They may be a preacher's child unable to meet expectations.
Remind them that hope is on the way.
Remind them that there is a thing called grace.
Remind them that Jesus condemned the Pharisee and self-righteous, and still does.
Jesus went to the unlovely.
Forgave the sinners.
Fed the hungry.
Healed the crippled.
Embraced those on the edge.
Struggling people are still on the edge.
Just don't let them go. Once you have them, hold them tight. They are at the edge because they were let go.

Some let go because they didn't want to be seen with those on the edge. Some let go because they saw those struggling as sinners. Some let go because compassion is hard.

Others held tight because Jesus holds the holder.

Christians sometimes get angry and yell at those on the edge. Christians today yell all too often.

Jesus does the opposite.

There was the woman at the well. Evidently a lot of things in her life were going wrong. Jesus even said, "You are right in that you said you have no husband, because you have had five husbands and the man you now have is not your husband."

Jesus didn't yell.

Jesus didn't condemn.

Jesus listened, responded with truth, and allowed her to realize the condition of her life and who He was. When she let that sink in, she became the first "apostle" to the Samaritans. She told those who would listen: "I have found the Christ."

Another time, Jesus spent all night in a boat traveling to get to the man of the Gadarenes. There was so much in this man's life that was out of kilter. He was demon-possessed, lived in a cemetery, and had no friends. Jesus took the time, came to him, and addressed the problem of demons. Talked. Sat. Listened.

The man's life was so changed that the men of the city now feared what Jesus had done and asked Jesus to leave. Jesus began to get in the boat that He had arrived in just a little while earlier. The man whom He had saved wanted to leave with Him.

"Jesus, can I come with you? Will you take me with you?"

"No."

"You can't come with me."

"Why can't I come with you? You are the first person who ever cared about me. You are the first person who ever listened to me."

"No," Jesus explained, "You have a bigger job than becoming one of my followers that stays with me. You have a more important role to play in the kingdom. You are needed here to do the work of God among the people who rejected you. They need you here! Tell them what GREAT things God has done for you."

This man stayed. The people listened. Their hearts changed toward the man who had been naked and living in the cemetery. They accepted him and listened. When Jesus came back, a massive crowd of people came to receive and welcome Him into their community.

The man of the Gadarenes had a great job, one only he could do. He was able to do it all because Jesus came to him and wrapped His arms around him and would not let go until he was safe.

Even encountering sinners, Jesus behaved differently than we do. When we see people who have scandalous reputations, we tend to avoid them. Jesus did the opposite. He embraced them.

A man hated like Zacchaeus was up in a tree. Hated because he took up taxes for Rome. He had become wealthy because he was Rome's tax collector.

Zacchaeus was easy to talk about. He was easy to hate. He

wasn't one of the tribe, so it was okay to hate him. "Everyone else hates him, so we must also."

When Jesus encountered Zacchaeus in a tree, not only did Jesus come up and talk to Zacchaeus, He said, "Hey, Zacchaeus, I am going to go home with you today and have dinner with you."

Eating with someone is a sure sign of fellowship. It was then and it is today as well.

Today, we invite friends to our house for dinner or to a restaurant. We don't invite our enemies to dinner at either place.

Jesus did.

When Jesus went home with Zacchaeus, Zacchaeus invited all of his sinner friends to join them.

During dinner, do you think there was an awkward silence for a while? Do you think there were questions about why He came to Zacchaeus's house?

If there was ever a dinner where I would like to be a fly on the wall, this would be the one. Afterward, there was a definite change of heart.

"If I have cheated anyone out of anything, I will pay them back four times the amount."

Something happened when Jesus encountered Zacchaeus and his friends. It seems like Jesus saw "sinner Zacchaeus" and grabbed hold and didn't let go until Zacchaeus was in a safe place.

Jesus holds them and you tightly.

Life is rough.

Life is tough.

Before someone walks quietly home from school, grab them and do not let them go.

Isaiah 40:11 says: "He will carry the lambs in His arms, holding them close to His heart."

CHAPTER 11

Communion

I was nine or ten years old. It was Sunday afternoon and I was with my grandparents, Nanny and Paw Paw. Surely everyone has a Nanny and Paw Paw.

Paw Paw took me into the living room. We didn't go in there often. We didn't sit on the furniture or bring any toys.

Well, we did go in there twice a year: Thanksgiving and Christmas. This room was kind of protected. The furniture was not fun to sit on.

Their car was child-proofed with this plastic stuff. It was everywhere. It was on the back seat. It was on the back of Nanny and Paw Paw's front seats. It was on the part where they sat, too. That plastic stuff was no fun.

Nanny and Paw Paw didn't wear shorts. My brother and I wore shorts all the time. That plastic and shorts did not go well. It was scalding hot from the sun. We always had these little dimples on our legs from the dimples in the plastic.

That Sunday that Paw Paw took me into the living room to talk to me, he sat me down on the couch to explain to me about church that evening. Someone from church had asked me to serve the Lord's Supper on Sunday night.

We served the Lord's Supper on Sunday mornings and then again on Sunday night for those who were not able to be at church in the morning.

Paw Paw told me so I would know what to do, where to go, and how to serve it. I never thought about it, but there was an order to how we served the Lord's Supper on Sunday night.

I listened. He was so kind trying to help me, a nine-year-old, understand what grownups had been doing for years.

So Nanny and Paw Paw got me dressed up in my Sunday pants, shirt, and shoes. I wore a tie. These were church clothes that Nanny and Paw Paw kept for me at their house.

Paw Paw took me down to the front row and showed me where to sit. Some of my friends came and sat with me on the front row. They had never done this before. It was nice to have them around me, but I was scared. I was so scared that I wanted to leave.

I had never done anything like this before.

My brother and I always sat with my grandparents. Well, they had to keep us separated so we wouldn't talk or play or giggle or look back behind us. I had figured out that you go to hell for looking behind you in church, because Nanny really, really, *really* didn't want us looking back there. "It was not proper."

Church was always long.

We had to sit still.

Our feet didn't touch the floor.

There was nothing to do except play with a songbook, so my brother and I developed a game using the songbooks.

Then Nanny found out what we were doing, and we didn't get to have a songbook.

I guess you go to hell for playing with songbooks, too.

There I was, scared, sitting on the front row with my friends.

The sermon was ending. My mind was racing.

I was to go pick up each tray in the right order. The person praying would ask those who wanted to take the Lord's Supper to stand, and then I was to take each tray separately to each person.

What if I dropped the grape juice and it went all over the floor?
What if I spilled the crackers?
What if I dropped the collection plate?
I had to take each of these to every person.
Nervous, scared, afraid.

Perhaps no one saw the bread tray shaking as I nervously delivered it to each person standing. None of the grape juice was spilled as this nervous nine-year-old carried it around. I don't remember if anyone put anything in the collection plate.

At the end of the service, there I was, relieved and still shaking. Then came the little ladies. They hugged me. The grown men came and shook my hand. My Nanny came and pulled me close and told me she was proud of me. Paw Paw told me he was so proud of me.

On the way home, I sat quietly in the back seat and felt a sense of accomplishment that I had done something that made people very happy. Nine-year-olds don't do that too often. We are usually stuck between grandparents so we don't talk, play, giggle, or look behind us.

A couple of years ago, I went to Jerusalem; it was an amazing experience.

I saw Gethsemane. I saw the olive trees. I looked from there across the Kedron Valley and could see the old city of Jerusalem: the walls, the shops, the cemeteries that surround it.

This small garden has ancient olive trees. They have been maintained for generations. Today they serve as a remembrance—of a visit and a visitor.

There is an Upper Room in Jerusalem.

It was in that room that Jesus gathered His disciples.

Those disciples were used to gathering with Jesus, but this

visit was special. It was different, but the same people gathered as they had done all of their lives. They gathered in this room to observe one of their religious meals, the Passover. The disciples had prepared the meal. Surely some of them always prepared their meals. They were together for three years.

While it was a traditional Passover meal, this was different. Something unusual happened. Jesus got their attention.

"I have been looking forward to this night so I can spend it with you. This is a very special night."

Jesus took the bread, then took the wine, and said words they didn't comprehend.

Dad had a flip phone. It used to be that Mom kept the flip phone. She kept it in her purse when they traveled. She only turned it on when she used it. She was afraid she would use all her minutes.

"Mom, you need to turn your phone on when you travel," we'd tell her. We would laugh because Mom kept forgetting to turn her phone on, which also kept us from calling her and using her minutes.

After Mom passed away, Dad learned to use the flip phone. Actually, he didn't learn to use it, but we could reach him with it. He did turn it on, though sometimes he forgot to charge it.

We all laughed at technology and my parents. Then we got my father an iPhone. My brother and I would visit and spend most of the time helping him understand how to use his iPhone. It tickled Dad to have an iPhone, and it tickled my brother and me because Dad would send us messages: "X34i st fp." Evidently, Dad was trying to send a text.

Dad learned how to call us, but then he would FaceTime me or my brother and aim the phone at his ear.

Advances in technology are hard to understand at times. I can't wait until some of my younger coworkers have difficulty using their flying cars or "jet shoes."

Here I am trying to predict the future. Whoever thought we would be talking into a watch? I should have known. I think Dick

Tracy of my parents' generation talked into his watch. We even had technology where Agent Maxwell Smart talked into his shoe and had a microphone in his ink pen.

Even today, we have difficulty comprehending Bitcoin. I don't get it. Some people evidently do.

As times change, some things stay the same. We struggle to understand things that are new to us—just like the time when Jesus said something that made no sense. A religious leader from Jerusalem came by night to talk to Jesus.

"Jesus, we know you have to be a teacher from God."

What? "We" know? What do you mean, "we" know?

We, as in the religious leaders?

We, as in the six thousand Pharisees of the day?

We? Who is "we"?

"Rabbi, we believe that you are from God."

To Nicodemus and those who are part of that "we," it was evident that Jesus was sent from God. As Nicodemus said that night: "No one can do these miracles unless God is with him."

Jesus and Nicodemus sat down and talked about God, about all kinds of stuff, but then Jesus said something confusing.

"Nicodemus, unless you are born again you cannot see the kingdom of God."

What?

Nicodemus had no comprehension of what Jesus meant.

"What, are you are telling me that I have to enter into my mother's womb and be born again? How is that even possible?"

Today we have the privilege of our time-goggles, so we can look back two thousand years and get it. Nicodemus didn't have our time-goggles. He couldn't wrap his brain around that.

Jesus even drove it home more: "Nicodemus, unless you are born again, you cannot ENTER the kingdom of God."

Nicodemus probably left there that night thinking, "What in the world have I just experienced?"

Change can be difficult.

There was another time Jesus was teaching and He made a very odd statement. With hindsight and some two thousand years to figure it out, we get it. They didn't.

"Except you eat my body and drink my blood, you can't have eternal life."

The crowd heard that and began to question it: "What? This makes no sense. How can we do that?"

What happened next?

That crowd of people who had gathered because they believed He was from God left. Walked away.

Their leaving evidently was so dramatic that Jesus looked to His own disciples, who had heard the same message. They had the same confusion.

Jesus looked at them and asked, "Will you also go away?"

Here are twelve fishermen, tax collectors, a doctor—all of them had careers that they could easily go back to.

"Will you leave me?"

Will you leave me, and go back to where I found you?

Will you also go away?

While they may not have understood the message, one so odd that the entire crowd left Jesus, Peter responded, "Lord, to whom shall we go? Lord, you have the words of life."

Peter, whom Jesus had renamed more than a year earlier, didn't have the benefit of time-goggles. He didn't know what Jesus was talking about. Peter just trusted Jesus to be who He said He was, a man like no other.

Peter had watched Jesus:

Heal the sick.

Raise the dead.

Give sight to the blind.

Feed five thousand people.

Peter trusted Jesus to be the Messiah Peter thought He was.

When Jesus was in the Upper Room, Jesus shared the future.

"One of you will deny me."

"Jesus, we won't deny you."

"Yes, one of you will deny me."

"Lord, I'll never deny you."

"Yes, Peter, you will deny me. In fact, you will deny me three times."

"What? This makes no sense."

Jesus took the bread: "This is my body, given for you."

"What?"

"This is my body, given for you."

"Jesus, you're the Messiah. You are going to restore the kingdom of David. You are going to bring back the kingdom that David established. David's throne will be forever."

"Remember? Jesus, don't you remember that?"

"Jesus, remember that James and John want to sit on the left and right side of you in that kingdom."

Jesus took the cup: "This is my blood, shed for you, poured out for you, given for you."

"What?"

Some things are hard to understand.

Jesus shared a cup of wine. "This cup . . . shed for you . . ."

Looking into that cup, Jesus had the ability to see battered lives, people losing hope. Looking into that cup, He could see widows who lead quiet lives in loneliness, children born into addiction and never knowing love, Jewish men and women killed because of their faith.

That cup held images of fathers and sons who live in uncomfortable silence, unable to express affection and never knowing love.

That cup held the images of unborn children because a mother lost her childhood and all of the violations that create pain and brokenness.

That cup held societies full of racial injustice that takes lives and divides nations.

That cup showed time from Eden to Gethsemane, and a humanity longing for a savior.

That cup showed from Gethsemane to the end of time where all have longed for a home, a place of no more dying or night.

That night in Jerusalem and later at Gethsemane, Jesus walked just as every man before Him—except this time, this man knew God.

As a man, Jesus must have seen all the pain, all of the hurt.

That night, He saw that He was to become the victim and the violator.

That night, He saw that He must become sin itself. He had to bear the cost of all who went before Him with the promise for all who were to come.

That night, He turned to His friends simply to be there with Him, though human companionship was no match for this pain.

It was in that cup, that night, that He saw that He must wait as Gethsemane became Golgotha. He must wait all alone even to the point that nature itself turned its back, the sun no longer shone, and the dead were no longer in sleep.

"This do in remembrance of me."

That cup . . . that blood . . . that grave . . . that curtain . . . that Sunday.

CHAPTER 12

If I Just Had Power

It was an interesting time in America. He was sixty-one years old. His wife had died. He had killed an attorney, Charles Dickinson, in a duel for speaking ill of her.

He had been in brawls in the streets of Nashville.

It was March 4, 1829, and Andrew Jackson was being sworn in as president. Four years earlier, Jackson had won the popular vote against Henry Clay and John Adams, but the Electoral College sent the candidates to the House of Representatives because there was no clear winner. Clay, knowing he couldn't win, threw his support to Adams. The House selected John Adams, America's political elite, in 1824.

Despite that painful loss, Andrew Jackson's supporters never gave up. They held parades, hosted dinners, and gained political support all through Adams's term.

On this Tuesday, Andrew Jackson exited the room and stepped out into a sea of Americans who had arrived in Washington to see him be sworn into office. Everyone wanted to get a glimpse of this man who swept the ballot, becoming the people's president.

He left his hotel room to the sounds of a thirteen-gun salute. His nephew, Andrew Jackson Donaldson, walked with him toward the Capitol.

As the president made his way through the crowd, social maven Margaret Smith described him as the "Servant in the presence of his Sovereign, the People."

John Marshall, on the steps of the Capitol, swore Andrew Jackson into office. Jackson kissed the Bible. The crowd was pressing, even overwhelming. There was a short address and then Jackson was ushered into the US Capitol, then out the west side. Jackson, dressed in black, mounted a white horse. The first populist president was on his way to the White House.

The transition was shocking to many, but redemption for others. The reins of power were just taken from the political elite and transferred to a common man.

It was a young country, but still held so much power.

Power.

Sometimes the transition of power is grand.

Sometimes it is taken.

Sometimes it is passed on more humbly.

Looking at power can be rather interesting.

Consider what happened on a mountain near Jericho.

Jericho claims to be the oldest city in the world.

It was here that I met Charley.

"Charley the Kissing Camel" was in the parking lot of a shopping center in the ancient city of Jericho. We parked the bus near Charley as I ventured out to look at an excavation site.

It was my second visit. This time I saw an ancient sycamore tree said to be like the one Zacchaeus climbed to see Jesus. Of course I went and took a picture.

Was it the same tree Zacchaeus climbed? I seriously doubt that this old tree was THAT tree, but that tree was in Jericho and we were in Jericho, soooo . . . maybe.

From there, our bus drove from the center of the city to a dumping area outside the historic community of Jericho. I looked out the window and saw another camel, but this one was not Charley the Kissing Camel.

Walking up to this unnamed camel that the shopkeepers had out for visitors, I looked off the edge of this deep valley—and saw tires, machinery, an old car, and garbage galore. A dump was beneath us.

Looking up from the shock of seeing the dump, I was overcome by what I saw before me . . . and it was not the camel.

Across the valley, standing on the outskirts of Jericho, I saw the most amazing mountain rising nearly straight up. On the side of this mountain was a big building or collection of buildings, built onto the steepest wall.

Why is that there? How do you get up there? How do you not fall off the side of mountain? How do you even get supplies up there, if people still even lived there?

One of the shopkeepers walked out to a group of us who were fascinated with the mountain and began to explain its importance.

"The devil led Jesus to a very high mountain and showed Him all the nations of the earth: 'I will give all these lands to you, if you will only fall down and worship me.'"

It hit me as to where we were.

Looking at that mountain, I tried to picture a tiny speck of Jesus on top of the mountain as the devil was trying to gain power. Jesus would give up His control of power, to gain ultimate power.

Everyone wants to rule the world.

When people try to rule the world, they can be ruthless. It was the same with Jesus and His encounter at this mountain. Jesus spent forty days fasting and praying for the encounter He would have with the devil.

The devil had control of the earth, but he wanted more. He wanted it all, total control.

We live in a world where leaders want "just a little more control." If I take this over, I'll gain a little more power, and if we take this country, we gain a little more power. Continuously, world leaders are building kingdoms with war and violence.

"I can make you 'king of kings' if you worship me."

"I'm sure you can do lots of good around this globe, if you will worship me. Think of the good you will be able to do."

That is a big temptation to anyone, because everyone wants to rule the world.

What a temptation! Each of us thinks it: *What a good ruler I would be. I would do so much good.* We might have to sacrifice a small bit of our character or a few human rights. We might have to take advantage of someone's weakness.

In the case of Jesus and power, He drew on the deep well of scripture. It is written: Worship the Lord your God, and only Him will you serve.

While we know that scripture is true, we know the good we would do if we ruled the world.

What you worship is what you serve. Worship power, and you will serve the devil.

In a world everyone wants to rule, men do anything for power. They fight back if someone tries to take their power. Kill the threat, win the war, rule the world.

Power makes sense. With all the power, you can control things. Imagine that world, where you have accumulated all the power. Oh, what good you could do it.

That is the way Jesus did it. Didn't He?

"Father, the hour has come. Glorify your son so He can bring power to your kingdom. Glorify your son so He can bring power to your people."

Is that how it went?

Nope.

"Father, let this cup pass from me, so that I can show your

power and retribution. Get even for all the things done to your son and show your power by getting even."

Nope.

"Father, take this cup away. Nevertheless . . . not my will, but thy will be done."

Declining the power.

Going to the cross, Jesus was not screaming hatred and promising retribution for all those who wronged Him.

"Father, forgive them, for they know not what they do."

Jesus went to the cross with no angels bringing retribution. No anger or bitterness.

Two men were crucified next to Jesus that day. One of them implored Him: "Lord, remember me when you come into your kingdom."

While hanging between two worlds—Heaven and Earth—Jesus looked at the man and wasn't angry.

"Today, you will be with me in my kingdom."

The devil had promised Jesus the world if He would fall down and worship him. But what the devil promised, God gave to Jesus.

Remember the crucifixion?

"Come down from the cross and we will believe you."

Jesus began to rule the world . . . from the cross.

"Let this mind be in you." Jesus emptied Himself and became human, obedient even unto death. And God began the power shift.

Oh, what a power shift; things really began to happen.

Power changed hands.

The light of this earth quit shining.

The most solid and stable thing known to man began to quake. In the holiest of Holy Places on Earth, the curtain in the Temple was torn from the "top to the bottom."

And most remarkably, the dead were raised and showed themselves to people.

People with power saw powerful acts.

People seeking a savior saw a death.

People went home wondering about all they had seen.

Rome was still in power. Hopes for the eternal throne of David died in the eyes of the powerful and the hopeful. All seemed lost.

Then there was Mary at the tomb, and a man she thought was the gardener.

"Sir, if you have taken His body away, tell me where you have taken it," she pleaded.

"Mary!"

"Oh . . . Teacher . . ."

It wasn't long before the remaining eleven encountered the risen Jesus as well. They worshipped Him, and some doubted.

Even in doubt, they kept worshipping. Jesus said, "All power has been given to me."

What?

"All power has been given to me."

"All power?"

"Yes, all power."

"We saw how you lost all power and even died."

"Listen to me, all power on Heaven and Earth has been given to me. Go into all the world and make disciples."

"Disciples?"

"Yes, disciples."

"What are we going to teach them?"

"Teach them to observe all the things you learned from me."

What exactly have we learned from Jesus?

Power?

No, love.

Not power?

No, forgiveness.

Why not power?

"No. Turn the other cheek."

"I think we need to teach about gaining power."

"No. Teach people about love, and kindness, and grace . . . those kinds of things."

"WHAT?"

"I have all power. I rule in love and want you to live in love."

Jesus was never pharaoh.

Jesus was never president.

Jesus was never Caesar.

Jesus turned down the opportunity to be an earthly leader.

Jesus has a kingdom.

His kingdom doesn't look like Moscow or Paris or Rome or Washington.

"If we can just get our guy in power . . ." we tell ourselves, "If we can just get our guy in the White House, then we can get the will of God into every state, make it be in every city and every home. We can accomplish what Jesus was unable to do in His life with our guy in the White House, or the Supreme Court."

"Just give me power."

"I will not be corrupt."

"If we had the power, we could bring peace, prosperity, justice."

With power comes zealots. With power comes their brand of religious devotion. Everybody wants their party to rule the world.

We have not learned.

We want to rule by killing.

We have not learned.

We want to make peace by using the sword.

We have not learned.

We don't want Caesar's sword.

We don't want Moscow's tanks.

We don't want Washington's money.

We want to be the disciples, a faithful church in all its power.

You are a city on a hill.

You are the salt of the earth.

You are the yeast in the dough.

You are the candle on a candlestick that gives light to all who are in the house.

You are the seed growing persistently through concrete.

We don't need to rule the world.

We don't need army tanks.

We don't need a sword of power.

We don't need the hatred that comes with rhetoric.

We have all of those today, and we see where it has brought us.

Our politicians are mixing Christianity with power and legislation to make people submit to Christ.

Lord, save us from politicians using your name to gain power.

The Lord's message was simple.

Show the power of character.

Live out the strength of faithfulness.

Share the impact of mercy.

Shine the light of love.

We simply need to be the:

Salt.

Light.

Seed.

Yeast.

The child of the King of Glory.

We need to be the children of our Father in Heaven, for He makes His sun to rise on the evil and on the good and sends rain on the just and on the unjust.

CHAPTER 13

Extravagance

One of the most amazing sites in all the world is the Church of the Holy Sepulcher, the traditional site of Jesus's burial.

God created a world full of extravagance.

Look at a snowflake. God could have made it a square or a circle or a triangle. He didn't. He made it extravagant.

Look at the human eye. It can see near or far. It can distinguish fire engine red from crimson red.

How about the human cell?

Each cell contains the DNA to re-create our entire human body and all of its intricate details. Every single cell is a world all to itself.

Consider the extravagance of a cell.

Consider the extravagance of a rainbow, made up of millions of water droplets scattered amongst a vast amount of sky. Things come together for just a brief, extravagant moment.

How about a peacock, or a tiny bluebird? Varying in size, they show amazing extravagance—one makes a massive show of tail feathers, and the other is tiny yet glowing in rich blue and red feathers.

Something as simple as a bird's feather shows unbelievable extravagance.

Look at the beauty of the planet Saturn.

God gives us such lavishness for a reason. He loves us . . . extravagantly. His entire message to us is love, and that love is extravagant.

We make rules that attempt to limit that love.

Stupid rules.

Mean rules.

Harsh rules.

We want to limit His love to us, or restrict that love from others.

He can't love *me*—not after what I have done.

He can't love *them*, not after what *they* have done.

Look at the way that Jesus showed us how God loves, with the parable of the prodigal son. The father didn't care where the son had been or what he had done or what he had become. The father simply wanted his son home.

Jesus gives us the Beatitudes.

We go back to Leviticus, with its rules. Lots of rules: Only us. We are God's people, not them.

We keep going back to guidelines given to Moses more than three thousand years ago. These rules were given for a different time and culture.

Jesus is telling us God loves us.

God loves us extravagantly.

God's people try to show a semblance of that love back toward Him. He allows us to love Him extravagantly!

Look at what Jesus did when Mary poured a pound of highly expensive perfume on His feet and wiped it off with her hair! Judas complained that it could be sold and given to feed the poor.

Jesus allowed her to show her love extravagantly.

"Let her alone," Jesus said.

She was preparing Him for a sacrifice that she did not even

comprehend—with the ointment worth a year's salary for a working man.

Jesus allowed for God to be worshipped extravagantly.

Jerusalem is filled with buildings that are man's attempts to show our love to Him. The Church of the Holy Sepulcher, extravagant. Whether this is or is not where Jesus was buried is really not important. The important part is that Jesus died, and wherever His body was laid, that tomb is now empty.

Opulent architecture throughout all of the world, all of creation, is our attempt to praise God extravagantly. To show adoration, devotion, and reverence.

Your worship may be as simple as a cappella singing or as ornate as a basilica in Jerusalem.

Your gift may be as simple as a widow and her mite, or as priceless as the art in a cathedral.

We worship a living God and attempt to show our adoration and devotion *extravagantly*.

Perhaps we do get it. Consider the love that grandparents have for grandchildren. We begin to understand God's extravagance when it comes to love.

*"Judgmental people are not fun or kind or loving.
I realized that I didn't like
being around that kind of person.
Then I realized that I was that kind of person.
That's when I changed."*

CHAPTER 14

The Life of the Party

Some of the funniest stories I know come from friends who rented apartments from me. They weren't funny at the time, but now I can look back and grin.

For more than twenty-five years, I have done real estate renovations. I buy a large, old, usually abandoned house or commercial building. I gut the building and start over. I'm doing that to a thirteenth home at this writing.

At one of my apartment buildings, there lived a group of friends who did everything together. When an apartment came open, they would call a friend to come rent it. Eventually, they filled the entire building. In this story, I will not use real names to share these friends' antics. You are about to meet Chad, the life of any party, loved by everyone.

One night around two in the morning, a renter friend named James called me. He'd been drinking.

"Frank, Chad is okay, but we called an ambulance."

"An ambulance? Why would you need an ambulance?" I asked, alarmed.

"Well, Chad thought he could fly."

"*What?* Chad thought he could *fly?*"

"Yes, Chad thought he could fly," James confirmed.

"Why in the world would Chad be thinking he could fly?"

"Well, we went to a club, we stayed too long, and Chad had a little too much to drink," James reported. "We got home, and Chad went in the upstairs part of the foyer and started singing."

"Was his singing so bad that you had to call an ambulance?"

"No. Chad said, basically: 'Hold my beer. I can fly!'"

"Uhhhhhhh . . . did Chad attempt to fly?" I asked, dreading where this story might go.

"Yes, he did."

"Yes, he *flew*—or yes, he *attempted*—to fly?"

"Yes, he attempted to fly, but no, he could not fly."

James, who lived downstairs beneath Chad's apartment, began to tell me how Chad's flight went.

"Well, he jumped . . . but, luckily, he hit the banister on his way down and that kinda slowed his fall. Then he hit a couch that was somewhere in the foyer and broke it. Then he hit the floor."

"WHAT?" I responded.

"Ohhh . . . here is the ambulance."

"Is Chad dead?" I asked.

"No. Chad was just drunk, or he probably would have been dead. He was kind of flexible as he hit everything on the way down. He is sitting on the broken couch right now talking to Amy from across the hall."

"So Chad is conscious?"

"Yes, he is conscious. They are putting him on a stretcher," James narrated as events unfolded.

"Do I need to come down there?"

"No, I don't think so; we won't be here. We are going to follow the ambulance to the hospital."

"Y'all don't need to be driving."

"Gotta go!" Click.

Bruised and embarrassed, Chad was released from the hospital the next day, a Sunday.

On another occasion, I received a similar call, also around two in the morning. And again, the story went from bad to worse as I fished for details.

"Frank, will you go get Chad?"

"Where is Chad?"

"Chad is at Krystal."

"Why do I need to go get Chad at Krystal?" I asked.

"Chad fell asleep."

"Okay . . . uhhh . . . so Chad fell asleep?"

"Yes, he fell asleep in the drive-through."

"Okay . . . and . . . ?"

"There was a police officer in Krystal."

"Okay . . . and . . . ?"

"When Chad fell asleep, he fell over in the seat of his truck in the drive-through. The cars behind him were honking. The police officer came out and knocked on the window of Chad's truck," Chad's friend said. "Well, the officer finally got Chad to wake up. He asked Chad what he was doing."

"Okay . . . and . . . ?" I prodded again.

"Chad responded to the officer by asking him where he was."

"Oh, this is not good. Sooo why did you call me?" I asked.

"Well, you're the only sober person we know on a Saturday night. They might turn Chad over to you instead of taking him to jail. Will you go get him?"

"Well, let me run down there."

When I arrived, Chad was in the back seat of the police car. I knew one of the officers. "I was asked to come down here to pick up Chad."

The officer handed me Chad's truck keys and said, "Frank, you can pick him up on Monday after he sees the judge."

This story ends well. Chad knew he had a problem and began working to change it. He moved to Nashville. I saw him a few years ago when I was there for a meeting.

"Frank, you will be proud of me!" he said. "The 'me' you knew before is not the 'me' that I am today. If I drink anything, it will be just one beer."

"Chad, that's great! Let me know if I can ever help you."

While abstinence would never be Chad's friend, self-control became a very good friend.

Around the world, it seems that alcohol and wine go with celebrations and gatherings of friends.

It was the same way some two thousand years ago.

At the wedding of friends, Mary became aware that they would probably run out of wine. Before long, they did. Servers looked around to see if some containers had been overlooked.

Mary went to Jesus. Imagine how that went. Music was playing; people were enjoying this beautiful celebration.

Because of the crowd and music, Mary probably spoke above a whisper so that Jesus could hear her: "They have no wine."

It was a time of desperation, but not like that of a dying child's father who came to Jesus for help.

This desperation was about a young couple and their friends having a party. Wine was important. When the wine was gone, the party would end. Knowing that, Mary went to Jesus.

Raising Jesus, Mary probably had to say some very firm statements. It makes me grin when I imagine Mary saying to a nine-year-old: "Jesus, do not go back down to the Sea of Galilee and walk on water . . . I don't care if no one saw you!"

I heard so many things from my mother.

"Don't make me come in there."

"If I've told you once, I've told you a thousand times."

"There are hungry children all over this country who would love to have some green peas."

My brother and I would always come back with, "Name three."

Growing up in the McMeen family meant summer evenings always played out the same way. Mom would step onto the back porch and say, "Y'all come on in the house, it's time to eat."

We would keep playing.

"Come on, boys, get in the house!"

We kept playing.

When Mom turned from the kind, sweet, motherly statements to demand mode—"Frank Turner McMeen Jr., get your butt in here!"—we dropped everything and headed to the house!

Mothers' words can be powerful.

When Mary mentioned the wine shortage to Jesus, perhaps it was more of a "Jesus, please don't let this party stop. Our friends are out of wine."

Jesus's first miracle begins to give us a glimpse into the heart of God. These people had gathered to celebrate. They came to support this man and woman as they began their lives together.

It was not urgent. It was not critical. It was a God of love celebrating with loving people.

God has always been this way.

Traditionally, church members sometimes believe that we should turn wine to water . . . or that Jesus turned water to Welch's.

Mary, without saying anything else to Jesus, went to the servers and said, "You do whatever He tells you to do."

Jesus kept the party going.

This first miracle, a non-critical miracle, began to show Jesus's true nature toward others.

The timeline of our lives is straightforward. We don't get to bypass the awkward, difficult, formative years. You must go through the first half of life to get to be the person you are on the back half.

In your first half, you work hard. You succeed, fail, accomplish. You develop relationships and build the person you are.

Without the first half of Chad's life, there would not be the Chad of the last half.

Everyone goes through the first half in order to get to the second half. Everyone has that awkward stage when we are extra imperfect, maybe prone to mistakes or actions that might seem out of character or regrettable to our second-half selves. So it's difficult to understand those people who seem to delight in condemning others.

I used to be that way. I condemned people who didn't believe like I did, didn't do things like I did. Then I found that I was drawing a smaller and smaller circle of friends.

Judgmental people are not fun or kind or loving. I realized that I didn't like being around that kind of person. Then I realized that I *was* that kind of person. That's when I changed.

While the former Frank might have been critical of Chad, my final words to him as the new Frank were ones of encouragement: "Let me know if I can ever do anything for you."

Along the journey of our lives, there ought to be a place where we know we can go for refuge.

I learned that I need to be that refuge for others.

Where do you go when you have totally screwed up?

Where can you find respite when the world is beating you down or beating you up?

There should be a place where those people blundering through their first halves can go to be nurtured or sheltered.

That place is often the least obvious place. Where do people go when life crumbles? Where do they find acceptance and love?

It is rare when people in our communities find refuge in the church. That is where they have found condemnation and judgment.

People should find the church to be vital to life. Sadly, it becomes the last place to do so.

Whatever our stage of life, the church should be our refuge.

You know it isn't. It is rarely the place where we want to go for help or even for celebration.

We celebrate with those who accept us. We seek refuge with people who accept us.

Recently during a lunch meeting, a friend said that churches are no longer preaching the truth because there are no hellfire and brimstone sermons anymore.

"People need to feel the anger of God," my friend said.

I disagreed.

I disagreed so strongly that it may have offended him.

"So, Frank, how do you get people to change? To repent? To be better?"

"My philosophy is, you love them so much that they become better," I insisted. "If your child is trying to learn to be a pitcher in baseball, do you yell at him for each time he doesn't throw a strike?"

I cannot imagine a Little League beginner improving with yelling and criticism. He would probably put down his glove and never pick it up again because it brought so much pain when he played the sport. On the other hand, I see that same child asking daily for Dad to come out and catch while he pitched—if Dad encouraged and helped him learn how to throw strikes.

A father or a home should be a place of encouragement and safety for kids. A refuge. So should the church.

Being involved in nonprofit work for decades, I never would have thought that the way to draw donors into my nonprofit would be by yelling at them or telling them how disappointed I am with their lack of giving to MY nonprofit.

Donors become fascinated with the work of a nonprofit.

I have a friend who feeds the hungry. Hundreds of people volunteer each week to help. So many in our region are drawn to the mission of feeding the poor.

Then there's my friend who helps the homeless have a place to stay during the cold winter nights. There are a great many people who help by volunteering to stay with the homeless and socialize with them during their evening meals.

While it is not for everyone, hundreds of people are drawn into the mission of helping the homeless.

Another friend runs a rescue for women who have been trafficked. Her fundraising events draw hundreds of supporters. Donors are drawn to help these women.

Volunteers become fascinated with the work of all those groups. Churches are no different from these nonprofits. People must find a fascination with Jesus.

Jesus *is* fascinating.

When church becomes all rules and religion, those who live by that mindset will find themselves irrelevant and declining.

People give by falling in love with the work of the nonprofit.

They love that children are being fed. They love that cancer patients are being helped. People love that they can help others who can't help themselves. People never make financial contributions when it's driven by criticism or condemnation.

The church is unique in the world. It always has been.

Why was the church prospering under persecution?

People living under the iron hand of Rome were fascinated by this thing called Christianity.

The church becomes relevant by creating fascination.

Early Christians were fascinated by the idea of hope, by the idea of loving your enemies, by the idea of a God of grace.

Jesus fascinated people throughout His ministry, but never by browbeating.

Jesus preached love.

Jesus preached differently from those of His day.

Jesus was life-changing, even without a miracle.

Why was Zacchaeus's home filled with sinners and tax collectors? Something about Jesus fascinated them.

The stories Jesus told have been beloved for generations because of their messages.

The story of the good Samaritan still teaches us to love our neighbor. The story of the prodigal son shows us that you can go home again. The story of the woman at the well gives us a message of hope.

Jesus would be condemned today as He was then.

Jesus turned water to wine to keep a party going.

That's not the Jesus many Christians have learned about from our pulpits.

Jesus went home with and dined with sinners . . . again, not something that preachers would encourage from the pulpits where I've been.

People who are needing Jesus want nothing to do with what they see in many churches.

Look back on the preacher who said what I had never heard before. He was doing what Jesus did. Whoever they were . . . wherever they had been . . . whatever they had done . . . Jesus welcomed them.

The common man was fascinated with and welcomed Jesus.

The religious leaders attacked Jesus because He didn't live up to their legalistic standards.

People flocked to Jesus because He fascinated them. Sitting with Jesus, they experienced the love of God not previously experienced.

The New Testament church was led by elders, not a board of directors. These first-century elders were living the second half of their lives having known Jesus and now were leading with the love of God they experienced in the first half.

I have a spiritual mentor who has helped me grow into the person I need to be in the second half of my life.

During a prayer of his, I listened and learned as he prayed: "Lord, give me the eyes to see people as Jesus saw them."

I have never forgotten that statement.

During a spiritual transition, I left a church where I had worshipped for a very long time. Nationalistic politics had become part of the leadership and bled into the pulpit, so I left.

As I mentioned earlier, I visited a church where some of my friends worshipped. My first Sunday there, the minister stood before the congregation and welcomed those assembled.

"Whoever you are . . . wherever you have been . . . whatever you have done . . . you are welcome here."

There is no way that this church believes that, I thought.

That day, worship was powerful. The singing was impressive, and the message wouldn't leave my brain.

As I was sitting with my friends on that first Sunday, one of the leaders came up to me during a song and said, "Frank, I don't know why you are here, but you are here for a reason. I want to pray with you about that."

He put his arms around me and prayed for the Lord to continue His work that brought me there that day. I had never experienced a prayer like that.

This church is different. It cannot be real, I thought. *This church is not normal. This church has Jesus.*

I was fascinated by what I heard. I wanted to hear more.

My visit to that church was so different from what I had experienced at other churches, I returned a couple weeks later with a sense of caution. I didn't want some razzle-dazzle religion; I wanted Jesus.

For most of my life, I experienced "combative churches." Yes, I had found some fascinating churches before, but it was rare.

Once I visited a college friend in Nashville. I got off work and drove to visit her and her husband at their church. It was a Wednesday night. That church fascinated me. The experience and the message would not leave my mind.

Back to Chad . . . there was a reason he and his friends were so close. They found in their group this feeling of friendship and love.

They broke so many norms, but knew their friends were there for them through anything.

On the other hand, I have seen combative Christians at combative churches. They were small. Their message was not one like Jesus would have delivered. There was no fascination.

Members left or fell by the wayside, or the church died out because they never found that fascination with Christ.

But then again, there are churches that make people feel like they are at the wedding in Cana.

I felt like I had been at the wedding in Cana.

People want to encounter Jesus and feel the same fascination people always felt around Jesus.

"You have saved the best wine for last."

Jesus turned the water to wine and put life back into the party.

Jesus fascinated the sinner and tax collector, Zacchaeus.

Jesus seemed to have forgotten to publicly condemn him.

Jesus touched the heart of the woman at the well.

There is a world wanting to encounter this fascination and feel this hope . . . no matter where they have been, or what they have done.

There is a world wanting to encounter this love . . . no matter where they have been, or what they have done.

The world wants a respite . . . from the world.

The world wants hope.

The world wants love.

The world wants a Jesus who would eat with them.

The world wants a Jesus who would party with them.

They crave a God who shows love rather than condemnation.

God has saved the best for last.

He's invited you to the party.

We all love a party, even God. So let's celebrate!

"We live in a temporal realm and in an age that relies on things we can validate with our five senses. We have become so fascinated by the things we have learned and verified with science that we may have lost our spiritual perceptivity."

CHAPTER 15

Alone at a Train Station

I had the most amazing trip from Anchorage to Fairbanks, Alaska, on a passenger train. What could be more cool than traveling through one of the most awesome states on a passenger train when you are in your early twenties?

I had been staying with friends in Anchorage. They were helping me adjust to the changing season and the expanding period of daylight.

In Fairbanks, I was going to stay with friends of theirs. Knowing people made it more special than adventuring alone.

The train ride was amazing. It was May and there still was snow on the mountains. Mount McKinley could be seen overshadowing the trees along the way. Most of the landscape was uninhabited, and no matter where you looked, you saw the beauty of God's creation.

The Fairbanks train station was not big. As we debarked, I was shocked at how small and historic the station was. Placing my luggage against a building, I sat on a bench and waited for someone to come pick me up.

The group of travelers at the station began to get smaller as the guests were picked up. I sat on my bench.

The station manager came out to me a couple of times to ask if I needed help getting anywhere. I told him that people should be here very soon to take me on my way. He went back into the office. I sat on my bench.

You could tell that it was about time for the manager to close up. He came out again. His policy, he explained, was not to leave anyone at the station and to make sure they had transportation to their place to stay.

"Who is picking you up?" he asked.

"Hmmmm . . . a friend of a friend."

"Do you know their name?"

"I have forgotten," I admitted. "My friends in Anchorage arranged for me to stay with them. I'm sorry, but I do not know their names."

"Well, let's call your friends," he said, and dialed the number for me. Ken answered the phone.

"Ken, I'm here in Fairbanks," I said.

"Great! You'll love it!"

"I don't remember the names of the folks where I am staying. I'm still at the train station, and it is about to close for the night."

"Let me give them a call and check on their plans," Ken said.

It was a few minutes as the station manager and I just kind of hung out. I don't think he had many travelers without a place to go when they arrived. They were used to left-behind luggage, not passengers.

It wasn't long before Ken called the station manager back. The college-age son was supposed to pick me up. He had forgotten that he was going to be my ride to their house.

The station manager and I sat on the dock as the sun began to set. He shared the station's history and how he ended up in Fairbanks.

It was not too long before a beautiful Corvette pulled up in the parking lot. A young man about my age jumped out and walked up to the train station. It was now dark.

"Are you Frank?" he asked.

"I am!" I said with a smile.

"I'm sorry for being so late. My family has been looking forward to your visit. I am Clint."

He picked up my luggage and put it into his car, a beautiful, new, shiny Corvette.

"I've never ridden in a Corvette before. This should be fun!"

"Everything is fun in a Corvette!" Clint replied.

I thanked the kind station manager for his patience and jumped into this amazing car. Of course we had to squeal the tires as we left the parking lot.

Off we went. Along the way, he talked about being in college in Fairbanks and about his career goals.

We talked about what it was like to live in the middle of Alaska. He asked what it was like to live in Tennessee.

Clint's family lived a little way out from the city.

The roads out of town were not smooth. Riding in a Corvette, you could feel every bump.

As we talked, the most amazing thing happened . . . the aurora borealis appeared. The sky looked so different, it was kind of scary. The green, yellow, and blue waves of light almost made this Tennessee boy afraid.

We pulled over and got out of the car. Mother Nature was in overdrive showing off; the entire sky was filled with light. It was like nothing I had ever seen.

Light in the sky is usually stars or the moon. We have lightning, but this experience amazed me. How in the world does the sky do that? Wave after wave of colorful light filled the entire sky above us. I was overwhelmed at the awesomeness of this natural Alaskan experience.

Remember the story of Mary, mother of Jesus, encountering Gabriel? She felt awe and fear. As Mary witnessed this supernatural sight, it strengthened her faith.

I was leaning up against a Corvette along this rural road outside of Fairbanks, Alaska. The aurora borealis is not rare, but it was not a common sight for me. Looking at this phenomenon, I think I felt a similar sense of awe and fear. I have never forgotten that night, that car, being forgotten and left until dark, perhaps all for a reason.

It all seemed to be a mistake, but the timing was everything. If I had been picked up sooner, I would have been inside their home. I might have missed God's amazing spectacle. I would never have remembered something as simple as the ride to Clint's house, which leads to this story.

This is a tale of faith, and how that night affected mine.

"We look not at things that are seen but at things that are unseen . . ." That scripture, 2 Corinthians 4:18, has always intrigued me. People are mortal and spiritual. Our life on this earth is limited. We are born and we die. We are also spiritual. We have a spirit. There is something about our nature that is spirit.

The scripture continues: ". . . for the things that are seen are temporal, but the things that are unseen are eternal."

So, does it say we see the unseen . . . we see the eternal?

Stay with me here.

The Old Testament begins the whole creation story: "God created the heavens and the earth."

Heaven/Earth.

Heavenly/earthly.

Spiritual/material.

Eternal/temporal.

God/man.

We get all that, but there is this mystery: ". . . the things that are seen are temporal, but the things that are unseen are eternal."

I get it. God in Heaven—heavenly/spiritual/eternal—created Earth—earthly/material/temporal.

We cannot see into the heavenly realm . . . or can we?

The Hubble telescope has revealed amazing sights in the heavens. Sometimes you wonder if some of the sights are perhaps a glimpse of Heaven.

If someone uses that remarkable telescope to try to find God or Heaven, it will never happen . . . or can it?

We live in a temporal realm and in an age that relies on things we can validate with our five senses. We have become so fascinated by the things we have learned and verified with science that we may have lost our spiritual perceptivity.

Some are so focused on the material that we cannot wrap our brain around the spiritual. If we cannot verify it by our five physical senses, we deem it as a mindless, religious superstition.

Perhaps we have become so dependent on the physical senses and our ability to document and confirm and validate, we lose this unique ability to live by faith.

If all we believe in is confirming and documenting—examining scientific *matter*, protons and neutrons and atoms, the elements that make up everything we can touch or feel or smell—then we will believe that nothing else *matters*.

But then we encounter God.

God doesn't follow our expectations. He never has.

God used the most unlikely boy to take down Goliath. For some reason, the shepherd boy, David, saw what no one else in Israel could see.

Perhaps David, underneath the glorious expanse of the heavens, saw periods of protection that could only come from above . . . after he fought off the lion and the bear.

God used a boy who was sold into slavery to save the world. Somehow, Joseph became the second in command of Egypt and saved the known world during a deadly drought.

Joseph never wavered in being able to see beyond this present realm. Something helped him develop an intense sense of character when others may have given into the world around them. Perhaps God opened his spirit to the heavenly as he was deep in a pit. Perhaps his spirit allowed him to see beyond the hopeless reality of his captivity.

There are times when God seems to open the curtain and allow you to see beyond this present world . . . if our hearts are attentive.

Children are born with a sense of wonder, open to seeing what others overlook.

"Unless you become like little children, you cannot . . ."

It was lunch and I sat down with a friend who was eating alone in a restaurant. We ordered, then talked and talked. Toward the end of the meal, she talked about her young daughter, who had been riding her bike with other children in the neighborhood. Her daughter returned as they were about to have dinner. She shared something one of the children had done.

Her mom asked, "Which child did that?"

"The girl with the blue bike."

"Frank, it was such a good feeling to see that my daughter saw something that most of us just cannot get past. She saw another child, without color. She saw the child with the blue bike instead of seeing the black child."

That precious child saw another child, her spirit . . . void of racial tones. She saw her simply as her friend.

Just as children have an amazing sense of wonder, there are times when God opens the heavens to reinforce our faith.

"We look not at things that are seen, but at things that are unseen."

Let's not forget that we have our life in this world, but we also have a spirit that is connected to the eternal world.

Given a sense of wonder, you begin to notice that the heavens do declare the glory of God.

Humans are amazing beings with abilities to climb mountains, run marathons, and design the most beautiful buildings.

Perhaps the most overlooked thing about humans is that we are body and spirit. Two different natures dwell in each of us.

Physically, a human can see in daylight and even at night. We can see near and far. As you get older, both grow dim. Our minds can do fantastic things. Our bodies, through exercise, can lift amazing weights. We can do physical things beyond expectation.

Spiritually, there is something that we seem to forget. We have a spirit, and that spirit is eternal . . . heavenly . . . beyond our comprehension. Because we are so physical, we overlook our spiritual nature.

Our lives are like interstates.

We zoom up and down the interstates of life.

We do not slow down. We find ourselves so driven by our lives, we fail to see the unseen.

This story is about faith.

"Faith is the substance of things hoped for, the evidence of things not seen," Hebrews 11:1 says.

Faith is the substance.

Faith is our response to the evidence that is given to our spirit by the unseen world.

How in the world does that happen?

Leaning against a Corvette in Fairbanks, Alaska, I was presented with a sense of wonder because the heavens declared the glory of God. That night, the wonder of creation shouted out to my spirit, revealing a glimpse of the glory of the spiritual.

You and I have friends who have been turned off to organized religion. Yet at the beauty of a sunrise or the majesty of a mountain, they will say, "This really speaks to me."

What happens there? When religion has turned them off, they are now listening as the heavens speak to their spirit.

It is amazing how the heavenly speaks to the human spirit.

The peacefulness of woods and streams.

The glory of sunrises and sunsets.

The amazing sight of a large, glowing, full moon showing the faithful existence of God.

When the discouraged experience this, they lean into it—experiencing the glory, feeling the heavenly, and finding peace . . . sensing God.

It is at these moments that we can discover a shining ray, or a beam that projects from the unseen world into your spirit.

We find, too, that in something as simple as the bread and the wine, there is a spiritual connection with the heavenly and our spirit. It opens the curtain to show us a sense of the heavenly, showing a God full of grace and love.

Awww, Frank, the bread and the wine are just symbols. It's just a remembrance.

No, my friend. It's Communion.

Communion is a breaking through from the heavenly realm into this world.

There are times when the bread and wine connected me to the point of tears. That bread and that cup connected me spiritually to the body and blood of Christ in the most powerful way.

Looking through the eyes of our God-given spirit, I can begin to make sense of the passage. Now, "faith is the substance"—the facts—"the evidence of things not seen" by my human eyes.

It is still a mystery, but I'm beginning to see.

May you use your spirit to see what God is revealing to you by what is unseen.

May He strengthen your faith, to give you peace.

CHAPTER 16

An Iron Lung and a Storm

It all ended in a bad thunderstorm in the early morning, long before sunrise. What a life it had been.

This woman wrote a book to encourage the parents of special-needs children.

She received a full scholarship from a one-page essay.

She received a doctorate.

She spoke at her alma mater's graduation.

Radio news personality Paul Harvey called me one day to ask me about Dianne. We had talked about her a little when he came to town for a fundraiser several months earlier.

Harvey wanted more information so he could feature Dianne in one of his *The Rest of the Story* segments.

Actress Jane Seymour brought her teenage children from Los Angeles to Jackson, Tennessee, so that her children could get to know Dianne.

Changing planes in a Florida airport, Seymour struck up a conversation with a fellow traveler.

"Ms. Seymour, it's a pleasure to meet you!"

"It's a pleasure to meet you, too! Where are you from?" the actress asked.

"I'm from a small town outside of Jackson, Tennessee."

"Jackson, Tennessee? I have a friend from Jackson, perhaps you know her—Dianne Odell," Seymour said.

"I do know of her, but never had the pleasure of meeting her."

"I'll be in Jackson in November for a fundraiser and will be her guest," she said.

"That is very interesting. I'll be at that same fundraiser. It will be good to have you back in Jackson in November!"

With that, the two separated and went on their ways.

Not only was the gala with Dianne and Jane Seymour a success, so was Dianne's sixtieth birthday party several years later.

Her birthday was a big event, with the who's who of West Tennessee gathering at the freshly renovated New Southern Hotel. Politicians, celebrities, and even Miss Tennessee were on hand to wish Dianne a happy birthday!

Just when everyone began singing "Happy Birthday," out rolled a nine-foot-tall birthday cake. The icing was purple and pink, her favorite colors. That cake was something else. It looked like it could have been made for someone from the world's oldest profession, or maybe made by a fabulously creative fashion designer—and part of it was. The foot-tall, silvery-white cake topper was handmade by a New York designer and shipped to Jackson. He had become a fan of Dianne.

Dianne Odell lived a remarkable life.

She lived in the days of Roy Rogers and Dale Evans. Roy came to town just to meet Dianne. Other TV stars dropped in, too, from the time she was young.

Who would want their children to live such a life?

No one.

Not one single parent would want their children to go through what Dianne did.

There was something unique about Dianne.

If you met her, you would leave encouraged. Many did—well, everyone who met her did.

Just ask Jane Seymour. She met Dianne and asked, "May I bring my children back to meet you?"

That is not what celebrities do. Celebrities don't meet common people and leave so affected.

Jane Seymour was touched.

But Dianne was special. She lived in an iron lung.

Jane was touched enough that she called Dianne and asked if she could bring her children to spend the Fourth of July with her and her family.

Jane and her two children got on a plane from Los Angeles, headed to Memphis, rented a car, and drove to the small house on the outskirts of Jackson. Spending that day with Dianne touched her even more than her previous visit.

Jane and her children got in their rental car and drove back to Memphis. The plane took them back to their superstar life on the coast of Malibu.

Jane came back time and time again.

Dianne never acted like a celebrity, because she wasn't. Yet, somehow, she sank into the hearts of those who encountered her.

One day, a thunderstorm came through West Tennessee and knocked out the power. That is a common thing in any southern town. Except this day, May 28, 2008, was different. A tree fell and the power went out. The lines were repaired, but not everyone was lucky enough to get back to normal.

Dianne had been stricken with polio at age three. As a result, she lived in an iron lung—a thing of a past generation. No one in the United States gets polio anymore. People don't have to deal with iron lungs anymore.

That night when the power went out, West Tennessee was changed. We lost our beloved Dianne.

Dianne had a generator, provided by the hospital system and the Community Foundation of West Tennessee. It was vital to Dianne and her house. It would kick in automatically when the power went out, except on May 28, 2008.

Dianne was sixty-three by then, and her parents were having health issues. That night, her father woke up and everything was quiet . . . too quiet.

Their house had not been quiet for sixty years.

For sixty years, there was the constant sound of bellows at the end of an iron lung, helping Dianne breathe.

Paul Harvey's *The Rest of the Story* was about a similar time, when an ice storm took down the power while Dianne was young. The power went off. Dianne's dad got up and began to manually force the bellows to make the iron lung help Dianne breathe.

Push the arm of the bellows.

Pull the arm of the bellows.

It had to be done. This was how Dianne breathed.

Word quickly spread. When the power went out, Dianne needed men to help the iron lung work. Everything was covered in ice outside the Odells' home. But before long on that cold day, a line of firemen and police officers stood waiting their turn.

They pushed and pulled the arm of the iron lung, helping Dianne breathe and keeping her alive.

Life is not fair.

Life is not easy.

A trip to Africa helped me come to the reality that we are blessed beyond anyone on this earth. I was there to help treat sick and dying children. Vaccinations and drugs helped them survive. Africa had few vaccinations and fewer drugs.

I don't remember the name of the small hamlet where we were. We had just met the chief and one of his many wives.

The church building and the mosque were next door to each other—two different religions, but everyone got along.

We set up our small clinic in the village's covered pavilion. There were only three or four of us. When I turned around, there were hundreds of mothers and children filling the little building and open area and spilling out to the street.

There was a sea of children and their mothers waiting for treatment of diseases eliminated from America. After several hours serving in our clinic, we ran out of medicine.

Dr. Pratt, our trip's organizer, grew up in Sierra Leone, just a few hours away. He looked up with tears in his eyes and saw so many children, but there was nothing else we could do.

In this open-air building, it did not take long for mothers to figure out that we were out of vaccines and medicines. Mothers were now crying with their children. They were pulling our arms and pleading in their language to treat their children.

We left that village on our way back to Sierra Leone. Not a word was spoken. We just sat there.

We were quiet.

Dr. Pratt, who has since passed away, had come back to his native country to help. Yet he was overcome by the suffering of humanity and by our inability to make much of a dent.

Life is not fair.

Life has never been fair.

King Herod killed every child under the age of two when he heard a rumor from visitors that a new king had been born.

Life was not fair.

Joseph was sold into slavery and ended up imprisoned in Egypt.

Life was not fair.

Joseph saved Egypt. He saved nations. Yet, a few generations after his death, no one knew him. The powers that be didn't remember Joseph and what he had done.

The children of Israel had become slaves for no other reason than politics. Now they ended up on the wrong side of politics. These once-powerful people had become the slaves of Egypt.

Life was not fair.

Life has never been fair.

Perhaps you remember the story of Lazarus, the man Jesus raised from the dead.

You may remember that Mary was Lazarus's sister. She was the one who poured the very expensive perfume on Jesus and then wiped His feet with her hair. She had sent word to Jesus that Lazarus was very sick.

A runner came to Jesus: "Sir, your friend Lazarus is sick."

Jesus replied, "This illness is not about death, but it is about the glory of God."

That made no sense to anyone there.

Jesus had encountered and healed children, the disabled, the blind, the possessed. Mary and Martha thought, *All we need is Jesus.*

Perhaps Lazarus had seen Jesus heal people. Surely, Jesus would intervene and save the day.

The runner came, delivered the message, and then left. No one thought it was a serious health problem, because Jesus didn't respond as people expected. Jesus didn't gather everything up and leave to go to Lazarus.

Jesus didn't seem hurt, shocked, or scared. He didn't do anything unusual. Jesus kept doing what He was doing for two more days.

For two days, no one brought it up. In fact, no one probably thought much about it. If it was not a big deal to Jesus, one of Lazarus's close friends, it was not a big deal to them.

On day two, Jesus looked at His disciples and said, "Let's go now."

"Back to the area of Bethany? Back to the area where they were trying to kill you? Why in the world would we do that?" they wondered.

"Let's go back to Lazarus. He is asleep. I need to go wake him up," Jesus explained.

"What do you mean he is asleep? If he is asleep, he is recovering. That's good news."

"No," said Jesus, "Lazarus has died."

They started the two-day journey. Jesus got close to Bethany, where Mary, Martha, and Lazarus lived. Martha heard that Jesus was coming. She ran to meet Him.

"Jesus, if you had only been here, my brother would not have died," she must have lamented.

"Your brother will rise again."

"Yes, he will rise again in the resurrection." She misunderstood.

"Martha, I am the resurrection."

Martha then went to get Mary, who ran to Jesus and fell at His feet. Following her were all their family and friends. They supposed that Mary was going to the tomb again.

"Lord, if you only had been here, Lazarus would not have died."

Jesus looked at her and asked, "Where have you laid him?"

Then, John 11:35, the shortest verse in the Bible: "Jesus wept."

Why in the world did Jesus cry?

This is the same guy who was told that Lazarus was deathly sick. Lazarus was sick enough for the family to send a runner to Jesus with one message: "Come save Lazarus."

Lazarus was going to die without Jesus. Jesus stayed two days, until Lazarus had died.

Jesus knew that Lazarus would die.

Jesus knew that He would raise Lazarus from the dead.

Perhaps Jesus was only fifteen minutes from raising Lazarus from the dead . . . yet Jesus cried.

Why would Jesus cry?

Four days after Lazarus had been in the tomb, Jesus knew what He was about to do. But Jesus cried.

Knowing that He was about to go to the tomb.

Knowing that in a few minutes, He would raise Lazarus.

Jesus cried.

Why?
Life is not fair.
Life has never been fair.
So, Jesus cried.
I am so glad that Jesus cried.
He saw people hurting.
Jesus always saw people hurting.
They were blind.
They were crippled.
They were hungry.
They were like sheep without a shepherd.
Jesus cried because *life is not fair*.

The Creator of the world planned on man living in a beautiful garden. He never wanted man to be here and dealing with death.

The Creator of the world saw our pain.

Jesus cried.

To show power over sickness and death, to show that the Creator had come to earth, He let nature do what nature does. In the natural world, people get sick and die. Lazarus died.

Life is not fair.

Jesus didn't cause the blind man to be blind, but He did heal him.

Life is not fair.

Jesus didn't cause the crippled man to be crippled, but He did heal him.

Life is not fair.

Jesus didn't cause the woman to have ongoing bleeding, but He did heal her.

Life is not fair.

Jesus didn't cause the sick child to die, but He did go with the father to the sick child and raise her from the dead.

Life is not fair.

Jesus did not cause Lazarus to get sick and die. He cried

because people had to suffer to see the power of God over death, the final enemy.

I am so glad He cried.

He cried because He can be touched when we hurt.

When life is not fair.

When loved ones forsake you.

Jesus cries because life is not fair, and people hurt.

When children die from cancer.

Jesus cries because life is not fair, and people hurt.

Jesus cries because life is hard, and people hurt.

Jesus is touched by the pain of humanity, by our problems.

Jesus cried because Lazarus died. Even though He was just minutes from raising him from the dead, people were hurt, and people were weeping.

Jesus wept.

Thank God!

*"You begin to see a glimpse of God in this:
What was once the ash heap and a place of sorrow
is now Bethlehem . . ."*

CHAPTER 17

The Ash Heap

When traveling, I tend to get off the regular route and see what is behind the curtain or on some back street.

While visiting the Upper Room in Jerusalem, I began to wonder and wander. I was with friends, so my time was limited as I began to explore.

I wanted to know why it was called the "Upper Room." I wanted to find out why it was upstairs. *What was in the lower room?* I wondered, figuring there had to be one. I headed down the stairs and through another door to explore the area.

Downstairs had a gift shop, a prayer room, and the Tomb of King David. Walking in, I was surprised to find it. The room had multiple sections. I had wandered into a room with a stone sarcophagus covered in purple cloth.

I have seen Napoleon's tomb. It was large, with an elaborate sarcophagus placed on a granite pedestal to prevent people from getting too close. The view was to project power and importance.

In contrast, King David's tomb under the Upper Room was rather simple. I slowly approached the velvet-covered, stone tomb with a sense of reverence. I joined others as they came in and prayed. Beside the large, stone tomb sat an attendant. She was in prayer.

My wandering sometimes gets me into trouble. That day, I was late returning to the group. My friends asked where I was . . . "Oh, I went down to visit the tomb of King David."

"What? Where was the tomb of King David?"

"It was beneath the Upper Room."

I think others wished that they had wandered off.

Then there was the time I was walking up the hill to the Church of the Nativity. The hill was steep. All along the way were the coolest tourist shops. I love tourist shops.

As I got closer to the church, I encountered the cutest child. He was maybe ten years old and was carrying a fluffy white lamb. I could not resist asking to pet the little lamb. I also asked if I could take my picture with him and his lamb. He obliged. That moment is among my favorites of all my trips to the Holy Land.

I continued my trek up to the church. Visitors formed a line. The stone, open area outside the church is packed with thousands and thousands of Christians on Christmas Eve. However, every day, pilgrims from all over the world visit this site, believed to be where the Messiah was born.

The lines are long. Once you approach the entrance, you find the church door to be small. It is only 3.9 feet tall, on purpose. Every person enters by bending low. Purposefully, the door to the Church of the Nativity makes every person bow as they enter.

After entering, you'll notice the rich wood of this historic church. Built in 395 AD, it is the oldest practicing church in the world.

The Holy Land has had a variety of conquerors. We normally think of Rome. There were also the Seleucids and the Persians.

When the Persians were capturing the Holy Land and destroying any signs of Christianity, this church was spared. The year was 614. The Persians were ready to destroy the church until they saw the large mosaic portraying Persians from the East . . . the wise men in Persian dress bringing gifts to the Christ child.

This beautiful, ancient church connects two worlds: our world and Jesus's world.

Because of Augustus Caesar's decree, there was an imperial census. Caesar wanted everyone to go to their ancestral hometown and register. Bethlehem was Joseph's hometown. Living in Nazareth, Mary and Joseph traveled ninety miles to register in Bethlehem. Imagine traveling to Bethlehem, ninety miles away, while Mary was expecting . . . *really* expecting.

During this census time, there was a shortage of rooms. Mary and Joseph found no place to stay. They settled for a hay bin in a cave in Bethlehem.

Bethlehem was first known as *Ephrath*, meaning ash heap or place of sorrows. Later named Bethlehem, it carried a much nicer meaning: "house of bread."

It was here at Ephrath—place of sorrows . . . ash heap—that Rachel, the beloved wife of Jacob, died in childbirth and was buried. Rachel's tomb is still located just outside the entrance of the ancient city of Bethlehem.

You begin to see a glimpse of God in this: What was once the ash heap and a place of sorrow is now Bethlehem, the House of Bread. Today the city of 25,000 is known for the birth of Christ.

Throughout Bethlehem, you can buy images of the nativity. It is on blankets, pillows, caps, rugs, and carved from olive wood. You can buy nativity snow globes. Every image is one of a sweet young lady having a beautiful child surrounded by cute, lowing sheep and wise men that came from afar.

What a sweet and precious image.

The actual story of the Word entering the world was not as romantic and peaceful as we sometimes portray it to be. Jesus was born in a livestock cave.

Having grown up on a farm with hogs, cows, and horses, I

have yet to find a stall or field or anything associated with animals to be sanitary. Sheep, like horses, pee and poop. Stalls never smell good, no matter how hard you try to clean them.

I cannot imagine that a cave where animals were kept was lined with the freshest hay or straw or anything. It's not a place where you would want to sit or sleep. Jesus was born in a dirty cave because they had no other options.

Just the fact that Mary and Joseph traveled to Bethlehem shows that Jewish people were living under the fierce Roman hand. Rome ruled completely.

Life was not easy. Survival was hard.

Jesus was born into a world much like today.

Our world has fierce rulers who control with iron fists. People struggle to survive.

Jesus entered into a fierce, mean, hard, and evil world.

Life is too often Ephrath . . . an ash heap.

Bethlehem was never a snow globe.

The world is rarely a snow globe.

When does life ever get to be easy? Those teen years are never easy . . . hormones, lanky legs, pimples, heartbreak. Young marriages are difficult . . . she doesn't cook like Mom, he wants to hang out with his friends. He forgot, she remembers. Careers end. An indiscretion ends a relationship.

Cancer . . . divorce . . . financial failure . . . losing.

Life always seems to be an ash heap. Yet . . .

At an ash heap . . . there was a glorious announcement.

At an ash heap . . . wise men nearly missed the birth of a King.

At an ash heap . . . wise men came to worship.

At an ash heap . . . came the King.

Jesus always enters at the ash heap.

Jesus always enters in a place of sorrow.

Jesus always enters at a place of desperation, even when you are down to the only place left . . . a cave.

The Word was made flesh . . . in an ash heap.

Shepherds were not expecting it.

Herod was not expecting it.

Cattle and sheep were not expecting it.

Do you feel overlooked, like you're living in a cave?

In the beginning was the Word. The Word was with God . . . and the Word was God . . . and the Word became flesh . . . and dwelt among us.

The Word will find you.

Do you feel like you're living on the edge of survival?

The Word will find you.

Are you all alone in the middle of a field?

The Word will find you.

Our Creator thought it important that the least—those at the ash heap—be the first to know.

Find your ash heap.

Sit there.

Sit in pain, and God will find you.

Sit there in loss, and God will find you.

Sit there hungering for love, hungering for *God*, and God will find you.

God will meet you there . . . at the ash heap.

*"So many things in our world
are upside down right now!
Maybe God is allowing this moment
to help us learn something."*

CHAPTER 18

Troubled Times

September 11 was a typical Tuesday. It was a beautiful, sunny morning in Tennessee.

I was in a friend's office planning an event when someone came in and mentioned that something just happened in New York City. We went into the office next door, which had a small TV. We watched smoke billow out of the Twin Towers.

We knew so little about what had happened. We were about to learn.

A small plane had crashed in New York before. This seemed different. As we watched TV, we saw a huge plane crash into the other tower.

What in this world was going on?

America was in shock. People cried.

The weekend came.

We were hosting our health fair, a large event that drew five thousand people every year. I was president of the West Tennessee Healthcare Foundation, which since has changed its name to the Community Foundation of West Tennessee.

At this regional event, there were doctors and health tests galore. If it affected your body, we provided a service for it. The health fair helped folks who could not otherwise afford it gain some insight into their health condition.

The time came for us to open the doors. We anticipated the usual long line around the building.

The line was short. People stayed home.

That health fair was so different. You could feel the uneasiness. Regular citizens were nervous, and they stayed home.

There was another time that left regular people with a sense of shock. We were still in the midst of the COVID pandemic, and we had just received some of the first vaccines. I was volunteering at our hospital, where people could come get a COVID vaccine shot. The lines were lengthy, and this daylong event didn't provide many breaks.

Someone saw a news alert. Sitting next to me, she looked at her phone and saw the US Capitol in the news.

Crowds of people were climbing the walls, breaking the windows, yelling from bullhorns.

America was in shock.

We pride ourselves on living in a stable country. We aren't used to rioting in the streets. We anticipate a smooth transition of power when someone else is elected. Instead, people saw unrest, anger, attacks, beatings. Congressional leaders were running for safety. People were troubled. They went to bed that night upset. People cried.

It had happened before.

John F. Kennedy was shot and killed.

America was in shock. People cried.

Martin Luther King came to Memphis to lead a march to help the marginalized. He was shot and killed on the balcony of the Lorraine Motel.

America was in shock. People cried.

Society is changing, and you may not feel safe. When the nation has lost its leader, what do you do? What *can* you do? Knowing that you cannot change what happened, you live in an uncertain world.

It happened with David, the beloved king of Israel. King David saw a threat to his kingdom from his own son. Absalom began his takeover much earlier. He began at the city gates.

"Did the king rule in your favor?"

"No."

"If I were king, I would have ruled in your favor."

Day after day, Absalom met with people coming and going into the city, winning the hearts of the people. He was charming and handsome, with long, beautiful hair to match his ego.

Taking advice from his two advisors, Absalom drove David from Jerusalem and slept with all of David's concubines "in the sight of all Israel."

Meanwhile, David encountered a man who saw the king leaving Jerusalem. He threw rocks at David and cursed him. David's world had taken an abrupt and unexpected turn.

What could the typical citizen of Jerusalem do when the king was run out of town? Those in authority were in disarray. Absalom had divided the kingdom and sent David fleeing.

Worlds become unstable, and the common citizen can do nothing but endure it.

Then there was King Uzziah.

King Uzziah was sixty-eight years old when he died and had ruled the country for fifty-two years.

He restored the kingdom of Israel to the glory it held at the time of David and Solomon.

Imagine having a ruler who was good, *very* good, and on top of that, his people loved him! King Uzziah was that kind of a man.

He was a godly man and ruled Israel well. His death left a void.

When they heard of his death, people worried.

"What will we do? Who will be our leader now?"

I remember when John F. Kennedy was shot in Dallas. It shook us all. The nation shut down for days.

"What will happen now that he has been killed?"

"Who killed him?"

"What kind of leader will we have next?"

The people of Israel had those same feelings. To some, Uzziah was the only king they knew. They loved him. They trusted him.

Isaiah gives us a picture of what was happening when King Uzziah died.

"I saw the Lord seated on a throne, high and lifted up, and the train of His robe filled the Temple."

Seraphim flew and cried out, "Holy, Holy, Holy."

What? I don't get it. What does this have to do with unrest and losing leadership?

Well, God wanted Isaiah to know that during a time of social unrest and questions, in a world void of leadership . . . God is still in control. We are still His people.

Governments are still in place by His choosing.

So many things in our world are upside down right now!

Maybe God is allowing this moment to help us learn something.

But with all this unrest, God wants me to know a truth I seem to forget.

In times of trouble, my faith may waver.

In times of trouble, I may lose hope.

In times of trouble, I may not understand the purpose of it all.

In times of trouble, God wants us to know that He is in control. We are His people. God does not waver when there is social unrest. God's love for us remains sure! His character never changes. Nor should ours.

May you still find comfort and peace when the world is not at peace.

CHAPTER 19

You May Remember Mark

Every community needs unsung heroes. Most communities don't have too many people who go above and beyond the call of duty, so it is rare when you discover one.

We had one.

Unsung heroes come in all shapes and sizes, and perhaps in all ages. I remember a small, "ruddy" kid.

David had older brothers, and they didn't like him. Because of his youth and his distance down the line of brothers, this kid was given the job of tending the sheep.

Day after day, he worked with sheep.

They were his life, because he was excluded from weightier family matters. He was not part of family decisions. No one looked to him for answers.

Unsung heroes probably have a character trait that makes them stand out. That trait is probably seen throughout their lives.

Something called out this child. It was the least expected thing that brought his character to light.

The prophet Samuel came to Jesse's house. God had sent

Samuel to find a replacement for the king. King Saul had become a troubled leader. He was vindictive, angry, and narcissistic.

Samuel shared that the next king of Israel was going to be selected from Jesse's sons.

Jesse was surprised, but delighted. He sent his oldest son, Eliab, into the tent to meet Samuel.

Samuel saw how tall and handsome Eliab was. He looked like a leader who could begin a royal line. *Surely the Lord's anointed is before Him*, he thought.

It didn't take long for the Lord to tell Samuel, "Do not look upon his appearance, nor on his stature, for I have rejected him. The Lord does not look upon people as you do. The Lord looks upon the heart."

Ouch. Okay. "Next."

Samuel excused Eliab.

Jesse summoned his next son. Nope.

Then the next. Nope.

Then the next. Nope. Nope. Nope.

Soon, Jesse ran out of sons. Samuel asked, "Do you not have any more sons?"

"Well, I do have one more, but you don't want him. He is out in the field, but David is not royal in nature."

"Bring in your remaining son."

Jesse sent a servant to the field and had him bring the boy to him. This boy, barely a teenager, came walking up to the tent. Samuel noticed this small, ruddy kid walking into the tent.

The Lord spoke.

"Arise and anoint him, for this is he."

That day, the prophet of God was told to anoint a small, young man who was not highly regarded.

The Lord chose David above the tallest and most handsome of candidates because he had something the others didn't have: character.

David was different.

David had not done anything out of the ordinary to single him out to his family or religious leaders.

The whole idea of character comes into play with heroes, especially the unsung ones. People of character do things that need to be done, but most people don't choose to do them. They may run out and rescue a child from drowning, endangering their own lives. They stand up for the oppressed, or go out of their way to stop injustice. People of character do things that others usually choose not to do.

Let's move forward a few years. David was still a young man, less than twenty years old. His father, Jesse, sent David to the battle lines to bring provisions for his brothers. Standing in the midst of the soldiers, David began to ask questions about the battle. He heard Goliath challenge the Israelites, and asked who was this man to defy the armies of God.

David's brothers heard his voice and became angry. "Why have you left your few little sheep and come down here? Did you just come to watch the battle?"

Some of Saul's men heard David asking questions of his brothers and sent word to King Saul, who then asked that they send David to him.

Before King Saul, David began to encourage the king, "Don't lose heart, sir. Your servant will go and fight him."

"Young man, you are not able to fight this Philistine. He is a seasoned warrior. You are just a small, young man."

"My king, I killed a lion and a bear . . . and this uncircumcised Philistine will suffer the same fate as them."

"Go, young man, and may the Lord be with you!"

There was something about David that gave him the courage to step out and fight this nine-foot giant.

The men in Saul's army failed to see the vision and understand something that David shared with Goliath: "The Lord will deliver you into my hands. I will strike you down and cut off your head. The battle is the Lord's."

That day ended with five smooth stones and a nine-foot giant being beheaded.

David didn't have to step forward. No one else was stepping forward. Anyone could have killed Goliath. David had something that made him different, that made him see the world and the situation differently from anyone in Saul's army.

During the deepest and deadliest time of COVID, a Tennessee man named Mark saw something no one else seemed to see.

He saw nurses and doctors putting themselves on the line, risking their lives to save lives. Those doctors and nurses were becoming tired and discouraged.

There was a time when the children of Israel were fighting the Amelekites. The battle was hard.

Moses went to a high place to watch the battle.

Moses raised his arms, and the Israelites were becoming victorious in the fight.

When his arms became tired and he let them down . . . that is when the Amelekites began to make advances in the battle over the Israelites.

Eventually, men came to help Moses.

They sat Moses on a rock, viewing the battle.

These men saw what needed to be done and came to his aid. No one told them to do so. They came because they saw a need. They came and held Moses's arms up so the Israelites would regain the victory.

Even when Moses was tired, the battle went on, with men assisting him. They held up his arms until victory.

Mark was there, like the men holding up Moses's arms.

Every day, Mark was in full view of every nurse and doctor who left the hospital after a long, tiring day.

Perhaps his efforts meant nothing to the average person driving along West Forest Avenue in Jackson, Tennessee, during the height of the COVID pandemic.

Passersby may not have noticed him, unless they were nurses, or dangerously sick, or doctors seeing dying patients all day.

Your town probably didn't have a Mark. I hope it did.

There's a reason most cities don't have a Mark. Other cities may not have had a person wanting people in crucial positions not to give up. In our city we had a Mark. Your city may have had its own Mark. I hope so.

Mark was there during the most difficult times of COVID.

He didn't do much but stand there and wave.

He stood there and gestured: "Thank you!"

The country shut down, but he didn't.

He really didn't have a reason to be there, but then again, he had all the reasons in the world to be there. Day after day.

He had one simple gesture, a wave of gratitude. He also had a small sign that said, "Thank you."

When the world retreated, he stepped forward. So did the nurses and doctors whom he came to save and to thank.

They were on the front line trying to save lives.

He was on the front line, too.

Nurses spent their days trying to save lives.

Mark spent his days thanking nurses for risking their own lives. One of his friends had a brush with death and spent several weeks in intensive care. This friend had a beautiful wife and three young, precious children who might not be able to see their father come home. A wife was close to becoming a widow.

Mark thanked those nurses for caring for his young friend.

One of the spiritual leaders of our community fought a hard battle but lost to COVID. Mark was there daily thanking those nurses who tried their hardest to save Clark's life.

Nurse after nurse pulled out of the hospital parking lot. Tired, as their shifts had become more and more difficult. Heartbroken at the struggles of patients. Encouraged that someone spent each day thanking them.

The nurses were paid, but never enough for what they were enduring. What Mark did helped them. He was there.

Then there was a day when we were there for him.

On that day, men came to hold up the arms of Mark and his wonderful wife, Carolyne, as their battle continued.

Mark became the one fighting.

Cancer is tough. Cancer is like COVID. It does not care.

His was diagnosed by accident, discovered when looking for something else. On this day, a group showed up holding signs and waving for *him*.

Just feet away from where he held signs to encourage nurses and doctors, he was once again on the front line.

But this time, Mark became the patient.

Men showed up to give him support.

Men showed up to let him know that he is loved.

Men showed up to encourage him not to let the enemy win.

Men showed up to give him strength to fight this long battle.

Mark is not a victim.

Mark is a winner.

Mark thinks like a winner.

Mark behaves like a winner.

Mark lives like a winner.

He knows what it takes to fight a battle.

Mark knows who will win the battle for him.

On days that were challenging, Mark remembered a small Israelite boy who faced a threatening nine-foot giant and emerged victorious.

On days that were difficult, Mark remembered Goliath's threat to the people of God: "You bring out this dog to challenge me?"

On days that seemed unending, he remembered the description of creation: "It was evening . . . and it was morning . . . a new day."

The darkness of each evening gives way to a glorious and bright day.

The battle with cancer continues.

Men are holding up Mark's arms.

Mark's battle with cancer continues to be a difficult fight.

In this battle, there will be no losers.

Everyone has learned a lesson from Mark, from David, and from the men who held up Moses's arms.

Because the battle belongs to the Lord. Either way, we are the winners.

God is good. He promises His children that we will overcome, in this life or the next.

Thank God for people like Mark.

"There are times when God speaks."

CHAPTER 20

Has God Spoken to You?

Samuel was just a boy. His parents had given him in service to the Lord. From the time he was a young boy, he trained under the priest Eli and lived at the Tabernacle.

One night, Samuel heard his name called out. Since only Eli and Samuel were in the Tabernacle, Samuel ran to the area where his mentor stayed.

"Here I am, sir. You called me," Samuel said.

Eli had not called him, however, and the boy went back to bed. Again Samuel heard his name, which woke him. He went to see if Eli needed him. The elderly priest told the boy that he did not call him. Samuel returned to bed.

A third time, Samuel woke to the sound of his name. When he went to Eli, the elderly priest realized it was God calling his young apprentice.

"If He calls you again, you should say, 'Speak, Lord, your servant is listening,'" Eli told the boy.

That night, the Lord had a special message for Samuel.

Has God ever spoken to you?

Yes, I know God speaks through His word. But has God spoken to your heart to do something that you know is right and what you should do?

Remember a time you had a decision to make, and you felt led toward a certain course of action? Perhaps fear of ridicule or fear of failure pushed you to ignore that message placed on your heart.

There are times when God speaks.

God brought the earth and sky into being . . . with His Word.

God spoke and His Word calmed storms, when His followers' words were cries for help in a storm-tossed boat.

God spoke to Elijah.

A powerful windstorm came. God was not in the windstorm.

After the wind came a mighty earthquake. God was not in the earthquake.

Then came a massive, raging fire. God was not in the fire.

In the midst of all that chaos, God spoke.

Yes, in the midst of the earthquake, windstorm, and firestorm, God spoke. God spoke calmly and quietly.

In a voice still and small, God spoke words to comfort Elijah.

Jesus once spoke powerful words to a blind man . . . healing words, probably very private words.

After putting spittle on the man's eyes, He calmly said: "Go to the Pool of Siloam and wash this off your eyes."

What Jesus told the man didn't create a large group of inquisitive people following him to the Pool of Siloam.

What Jesus said was not loud and echoing through the countryside. It was simple.

When Jesus said to go wash in the Pool of Siloam, the blind man went. He washed off his eyes and came home seeing.

Listening to Jesus created quite an earthquake, quite a firestorm, quite a windstorm.

There was a time when the earthquake, the firestorm, and the windstorm came to Jesus.

This time, Jesus went to the Temple. The Pharisees, seeing Jesus, brought a woman to Him.

"Jesus, you claim to be such a great teacher. We have a sinner here, a woman caught in adultery. The law says stone her . . . what do you say?"

From this point on, the story gets personal.

Jesus knew they were there only for political purposes. Yes, political purposes. They did not care about her; they were simply doing some political maneuvering.

Knowing that, Jesus knelt down and began writing in the dirt.

When Jesus didn't respond, they became more insistent: "Jesus, you great teacher, please tell us what we need to do! We have caught this woman in the act of adultery. What should we do?"

Jesus kept writing in the dirt.

"Oh, great teacher! Jesus, you are acclaimed as such a great teacher, tell us what we should do. She was caught in adultery, in the very act. The law says stone her. Should we stone her?"

We seem to forget the audience that had gathered to hear the teachings of Jesus that day. A crowd had gathered at the Temple, the logical place for the Pharisees to feel right at home.

"Come on, Jesus! What should we do?"

That day, there were two people down on the ground: the woman caught in adultery and Jesus.

Jesus stood up from writing in the dirt.

"Sure, stone her. Go ahead. But those of you who have never sinned, you must be the first to start the stoning."

Jesus stooped back down and wrote in the dirt. He was over their hypocritical actions and knelt again next to the woman.

What Jesus wrote is of no importance. What Jesus *said* was a bombshell.

Without saying a word, the Pharisees and their political players slowly disappeared into the Temple crowd.

Amazingly, there were no more Pharisees in the group. They

had whimpered away and it was just Jesus, the woman, and the huge crowd that had gathered.

Jesus stood up and asked *her* . . . "Woman, where are your accusers?"

"They have gone, sir."

Looking into her eyes, Jesus didn't use an earthquake. Jesus didn't use a great wind or firestorm from Heaven.

Jesus probably stepped closer to speak to her, to tell her He did not condemn her. She must have felt the presence of God as she listened to His still, small voice. The message likely echoed deep in her soul: "You beautiful child . . . you are important in the eyes of God, so live like you know who you are!"

Look at the earthquakes in our cultures.

Look at the firestorms in our cities.

Look at the windstorms shaking our belief systems.

God is speaking to *you* . . . in a still, small voice.

Isaiah was given a vision during a very troubling time for Israel. The king, Uzziah, had died after reigning for more than fifty years. He was the only ruler whom many Israelites had ever known. He was a good king for the people, but his death created uncertainty.

Isaiah was given this vision . . . one of Heaven.

The world was falling apart. People were scared.

During a time of stress and uncertainty, Isaiah was given a vision of Heaven for a reason. The Lord wanted him and all of Israel to know that nothing had changed.

God was still on His throne. Although the world was on fire, God was still in control.

He was telling Israel: *My messages are true.*

He was telling Israel: *My love will not waver.*

These are powerful messages that He still is sending to you. He always has spoken to you.

God's character has not changed.

His love for humanity has not wavered.

We should not let the noise of the earthquake or windstorm or firestorm prevent us from hearing Him.

He is still speaking.

His message is there even when you are not listening.

His message is one of love.

His message is one for all people.

His message is to people you may exclude from society.

His message is to people you may exclude from church.

Can you hear Him speaking His message to you?

Dr. Frank McMeen

For more than two decades, Dr. Frank McMeen has served as president of the Community Foundation of West Tennessee (formerly known as the West Tennessee Healthcare Foundation) in Jackson, Tennessee. He's a former vice president of university advancement at Freed-Hardeman University, past president of Columbia Academy, and was an adjunct faculty member at the University of Memphis and Freed-Hardeman University. He has served as president of the Lambuth Area Neighborhood Association off and on for more than ten years, and he was elected to Jackson's City Council.

He serves on numerous local boards, including the Boys & Girls Club, Jackson Equity Project, and the Jackson Rotary Club. He is the treasurer of the Tennessee Dental Association Foundation and served as president of the Association for the Preservation of Tennessee Antiquities.

He enjoys historic preservation and is restoring his thirteenth historic home in Jackson. He loves animals and rescued his dogs, Bonnie May, Lucky Dawg, and Minnie Mutt. He worships at Skyline Church. He was raised on a farm outside Columbia, Tennessee, where walking horses were a vital part of his life, with his father winning two world grand championships.

It's All about a Story: Be Encouraged is McMeen's second book. His first was *Let Me Tell You a Story: Finding Hope in a Hopeless World*.